JavaScript

PROGRAMMER'S REFERENCE

Christian MacAuley
Paul Jobson

Osborne/**McGraw-Hill**

New York Chicago San Francisco
Lisbon London Madrid Mexico City Milan
New Delhi San Juan Seoul Singapore Sydney Toronto

Osborne/**McGraw-Hill**
2600 Tenth Street
Berkeley, California 94710
U.S.A.

To arrange bulk purchase discounts for sales promotions, premiums, or
fund-raisers, please contact Osborne/**McGraw-Hill** at the above address.
For information on translations or book distributors outside the U.S.A.,
please see the International Contact Information page immediately
following the index of this book.

JavaScript Programmer's Reference

Publisher   Brandon A. Nordin
Vice President & Associate Publisher   Scott Rogers
Acquisitions Editor   Ann Sellers
Project Editor   Julie M. Smith
Acquisitions Coordinators   Paulina Pobocha & Timothy Madrid
Technical Editor   Pankaj Kamtham
Copy Editor   Judith Brown
Proofreader   Linda Medoff
Computer Designers   Tara A. Davis & George Toma Charbak
Illustrators   Michael Mueller & Lyssa Wald
Series Design   Peter F. Hancik

1234567890 DOC DOC 01987654321

ISBN 0-07-219296-8

This book was composed with Corel VENTURA™ Publisher.

About the Authors

Christian MacAuley is a web coder, designer, writer, and trainer. Her extensive experience as a JavaScript coder in the streaming media industry has garnered her clients such as PSINet, eStackig, and TV on the Web, among others. Christian's articles about web design and coding have appeared in *Web Review* and *ArtToday*. Christian is also the author of *Palm Handhelds for Visual Learners* (VisiBooks 2001).

Paul Jobson has been building web sites since 1994 and has extensive experience coding client-side JavaScript, Dynamic HTML, and Perl. He is currently contracting for a Fortune 50 company in the DC Metro area.

CONTENTS

Appendix

Index

ACKNOWLEDGMENTS

We would like to thank Ann Sellers, Julie Smith, Tim Madrid, Paulina Pobocha and Tara Davis from Osborne-McGraw-Hill for putting up with our delays and helping us along. Thanks to our parents and friends who gave us support, especially: Keith, Ranjit, Kate, and Sheridan.

INTRODUCTION

JavaScript is a must-have tool for web developers creating dynamic web sites in the 21st century. As well as being a useful tool for server-side scripting, JavaScript has become the most popular and widely supported client-side scripting language for the World Wide Web.

Although JavaScript has a reputation for being a simple programming language, that's only partly true. JavaScript is complicated enough for serious programmers to use for serious jobs, yet simple enough for non-programmers to use to plug basic interactivity into to web pages.

Another common misconception about JavaScript is that it's a subset of the Java programming language. In reality the only connection between Java and JavaScript is that they are both open, cross-platform languages capable of working with one another.

Although JavaScript isn't Java, JavaScript's syntax is similar to object oriented programming languages like Java and C++. This makes the language easy for object-oriented programmers to pick up. Although you don't have to be a Java or C++ programmer to use either JavaScript or this book, you should be familiar with how programming works and the different kinds of tasks client-side and server-side scripts perform on web sites.

Since Netscape Communications announced JavaScript in 1995, the language has undergone a lot of changes and come a long way. The original JavaScript 1.0 is virtually obsolete, and version numbers have climbed as high as JavaScript 1.5. JavaScript has also spawned different implementations such as JScript by Microsoft and the standardized ECMA script by the European Computer Makers Association. We feel that JavaScript will continue to evolve and to meet the changing needs of web applications.

Chapter 1
Core JavaScript

This chapter discusses JavaScript's core language conventions, including case sensitivity, keywords, data types, reserved words, and operators to get you rolling if you're new to JavaScript.

Language Conventions

Case Sensitivity

Core JavaScript language is case sensitive. This means keywords, variables, function names, or any other identifiers must contain exactly the same letters in the same case. The variable `SomeVariable` is not the same as `SOMEVARIABLE`, which is not the same as `somevariable`.

Microsoft's Internet Explorer browser is the only deviant from this rule. In Internet Explorer, Core JavaScript is case sensitive, but any objects, and their methods and properties, that are added by the Client-Side JavaScript are not case sensitive. For example, `Date()` and `Math()` are Core JavaScript functions, and therefore it is invalid to write them as `date()`, `DATE()`, `Math()`, or `mAth()`. On the other hand, the `form` object is part of Client-Side JavaScript, and therefore it is valid to write it as `window.form` or `window.FORM` or `window.Form`. Remember, these rules apply to Internet Explorer only and it's not good practice to ignore cases.

Code Formatting

Line Breaks and Whitespace
JavaScript ignores line breaks and whitespace, except in strings and tokens. Whitespace represents a space or tab. Tokens are defined as keywords, variable names, numbers, function names, or some place that you wouldn't want a line break or whitespace. A token could be the number `2002`; if you added a space, the numbers `200 2` would be considered two tokens.

Semicolons

JavaScript, like many programming languages, has semicolons at the end of statements. Still, JavaScript does not require you to put a semicolon at the end of a statement. Each of the following statements is valid:

```
ThisMonth = "August"
someyear = "2022";
nextnum = 33;
        testvalue = 300
```

If there are several statements on one line, you must use semicolons:

```
thisyear = "2001"; othernum = 100;
```

Even though semicolons are optional, it is better coding practice not to omit them.

Comments

JavaScript comments are simply notes within the code—and they are not part of the program. Developers (such as you) generally use comments to add notes to the code for later reference. There are two forms of comments in JavaScript. Line comments begin with // and end with a line break, and multiline comments begin with /* and end with */. Several lines may fall between these symbols.

```
// This is a comment
num = 5; // Comments may follow a line of code.
/* Comments may span several lines,
as long as you use this kind of commenting */
```

Literals and Identifiers

A literal represents a value in JavaScript. Literals are fixed values, not variables, which you define. Several types of literals are integer literals, octal literals, hexadecimal literals, and string literals.

Reserved Words

In JavaScript there are several groups of words that fall into the "reserved word" category. Reserved words are words that you should not use as identifiers. You may not use any JavaScript

break	false	this
in	void	continue
for	new	true
while	delete	function
null	var	typeof
with	else	return
if		

Table 1-1.   JavaScript Keywords

keywords, shown in Table 1-1. JavaScript keywords are part of the language syntax, so they should be avoided. Also, Java keywords, displayed in Table 1-2, should be avoided. Java keywords are not yet used in JavaScript, but future versions of JavaScript may use them. Table 1-3 lists other identifiers to be avoided—these are names of data types, functions, and variables that are predefined by Client-Side JavaScript. Since Internet Explorer is not case sensitive, all keywords in Table 1-2 should be avoided in lowercase and uppercase. Finally, there are words reserved for possible future extensions to the ECMA-262 standard, which are shown in Table 1-4.

abstract	default	implements
private	throw	boolean
do	import	protected
throws	byte	double
instanceof	public	transient
case	extends	int
short	try	catch
final	interface	static
char	finally	long
class	float	native
switch	const	goto
package	synchronized	super

Table 1-2.   Java Keywords

alert	escape	JavaPackage
onunload	setTimeout	Anchor
eval	length	open
status	Area	FileUpload
Link	opener	String
Array	focus	Location
Option	Submit	assign
Form	location	Packages
sun	blur	Frame
Math	parent	taint
Boolean	frames	MimeType
parseFloat	Text	Button
Function	name	parseInt
Textarea	Checkbox	getClass
navigate	Password	top
clearTimeout	Hidden	Navigator
Plugin	toString	close
History	navigator	prompt
unescape	closed	history
netscape	prototype	untaint
confirm	Image	Number
Radio	valueOf	Date
isNaN	Object	ref
Window	defaultStatus	java
onblur	Reset	window
Document	JavaArray	onerror
scroll	document	JavaClass
onfocus	Select	Element
JavaObject	onload	self
callee	caller	

Table 1-3. Other Identifiers to Be Avoided

catch	const	enum
finally	throw	class
debugger	extends	super
try		

Table 1-4.   ECMA Extensions

Data Types

Numbers

Numbers are basic data types; numeric literals may be integer or floating point; and integers may be decimal, octal, or hexadecimal. JavaScript does not make a distinction between floating-point and integer values; JavaScript recognizes all numbers as floating-point values. These floating-point numbers may be represented as large as $+/- 1.7976931348623157 \text{x} 10^{308}$ and as small as $+/- 5 \text{x} 10^{-324}$.

Integer Literals

Integer literals are represented by Base-10 numbers, which are positive or negative numbers that do not begin with a zero. Integer literals never have decimals, for example,

```
32
```

```
61245
```

```
-128r43
```

```
1584
```

Octal and Hexadecimal Literals

Integer literals may also be represented by octal (Base-8) and hexadecimal (Base-16) values. Octal literals are positive or negative numbers from 0 through 7, which may begin with a 0. For example, the following numbers are octal literals:

```
030547

-447

56027
```

Hexadecimal literals are positive or negative numbers that begin with 0x or 0X and are followed by either numbers 0 through 9 and/or letters A through F. The letters A through F represent the numbers 10 through 15 and are case insensitive. For example, the following numbers are hexidecimal literals:

```
-0x21548FFAD

0Xabafd65484

0xABCD

-0x1234
```

Floating-Point Literals

Floating-point literals are positive or negative numbers, that may or may not have decimals. They also may include positive or negative exponents, which follow the letter E. For example, the following numbers are floating-point literals:

```
5.0153

-24.563

.13546984

-.6546
```

```
45.0687E+52
```

```
546.468E-54
```

Special Numeric Values

Special numeric values are used during several events. If a floating-point value is larger than the largest number available, it will return `Infinity`. Inversely, if a floating-point value is lower than the most negative number, the value will be returned as `-Infinity`. Several mathematical operations, such as division by zero, result in Not-a-Number, which is printed as `NaN`. Not-a-Number does not compare equally to any other number, including itself. A function called `isNaN()` is used to test for `NaN`. There are constants defined for each of these special numeric values, as shown in Table 1-5.

For more information on special numeric values, see the Number object in Chapter 4.

Strings

A string is simply a sequence of letters, numbers, punctuation marks, and so on. It is a data type containing text.

String Literals

String literals contain any number of characters, including zero, contained within single or double quotes. Double quote strings may be contained in single quote strings, as in the next.

Constant	Meaning
`Number.MAX_VALUE`	Largest representable number
`Number.MIN_VALUE`	Most negative representable number
`Number.NaN`	Special Not-a-Number value
`Number.POSITIVE_INFINITY`	Special value to represent infinity
`Number.NEGATIVE_INFINITY`	Special value to represent negative infinity

Table 1-5.   Special Numeric Constants

```
"This is a string."
"465.654"
'This is a test'
'value="10"'
```

Escape Sequences in String Literals

Escape sequences always start with a backslash \. See Table 1-6 for each escape sequence.

The escape sequence listed as \xxx in Table 1-6 represents the character with the Latin-1 (ISO-8859-1) encoding. These sequences are used to represent characters not found on a standard keyboard. For example, the \174 sequence represents the Registered symbol ®.

Boolean Literals

Boolean literals represent a logical value, either true or false. These values are used in comparisons to determine whether the

Sequence	Character Represented
\b	Backspace
\f	Form feed
\n	Newline
\r	Carriage return
\t	Tab
\'	Apostrophe or single quote
\"	Double quote
\\	Backslash
\xxx	The character with the Latin-1 encoding; contains one to three octal digits, between 0 and 377
\xXX	The character with the Latin-1 encoding; contains two hexadecimal digits, between 00 and FF
\uXXXX	The Unicode character, specified by four hexadecimal characters (not supported by Netscape 4)

Table 1-6. Escape Sequence Definitions

comparison is valid or invalid (true or false). Boolean literals are commonly used in `while` loops, like the following:

```
while(test = true) {
      doSomething()
      if (num != 1) test = false;
      }
```

Other Values

The `null` Literal   The keyword `null` represents a lack of value, while each of the other literals represents some kind of value. In JavaScript, unlike several other programming languages, `null` is not equal to 0.

undefined   undefined is not the same as `null`. The undefined value is returned when you use a variable that does not exist or a variable that has been declared but has not been assigned a value.

Variables

"Untyped" Variables

JavaScript is a dynamically typed language, which means you do not have to specify the data type of a variable when you declare it. The data types are converted as needed during the execution of the script.

For example, you could define the following variable:

```
var images = 100;
```

Later, you could change from a numeric value to a string value:

```
images = "We have many images.";
```

This would not return an error, because JavaScript is dynamically typed.

Declaring Variables

A variable can be assigned in three ways. You can implicitly declare a variable by simply assigning it a value, for example,

```
x = 12; // declaring and assigning a value to x
```

Or you can explicitly declare a variable using the `var` keyword. Using `var`, assigning a value is optional. If you don't assign a value to your variable, the value will be `undefined`.

```
var x; // simply declaring x
var x = 12; // declaring and assigning a value to x
```

Operators

On the following pages, we'll discuss each JavaScript operator in detail. The operators used in JavaScript are very similar to those used in C++ and Java. Table 1-7 provides an overview of the operators available in JavaScript, what each operator does, and which operands each operator expects.

Operator	Operand(s) Type	Summary of Operation	Notes
+	Numbers, strings	Adds numbers, concatenates strings	
+=	Numbers, strings	Adds second number to first, assigns new value; concatenates strings and assigns new value	
++	Numbers	Pre- or post-increments	
–	Numbers	Subtracts	
–=	Numbers	Subtracts second operand from first, assigns new value	
«--	Numbers	Pre- or post-decrements	
*	Numbers	Multiplies	
/	Numbers	Divides first operand by second	
/=	Numbers	Divides first operand by second, assigns new value	
%	Numbers	Divides for remainder	

Table 1-7. Summary of Operators

Operator	Operand(s) Type	Summary of Operation	Notes
%=	Numbers	Divides for remainder, assigns a new value	
<	Numbers or strings	Tests numbers for less than, tests strings for ABC order	
<=	Numbers or strings	Tests numbers for less than or equal to, tests strings for ABC order	
>	Numbers or strings	Tests numbers for greater than, tests strings for ABC order	
>=	Numbers or strings	Tests numbers for greater than or equal to, tests strings for ABC order	
==	Any	Tests for equality	Some inconsistencies in Netscape
===	Any	Tests for same identity	JavaScript 1.3 and higher
!	Boolean	Returns logical complement of single operand	
!=	Any	Tests for inequality	
!==	Any	Tests for same identity	JavaScript 1.3 and higher
&&	Booleans	Tests for logical AND	
||	Booleans	Tests for logical OR	
,	Any	Evaluates two statements	
.	Object, property, method	Accesses object properties and methods	
[]	Array, integer	Accesses an array index	
()	Function, arguments	Performs a function call	

Table 1-7.   Summary of Operators *(continued)*

Operator	Operand(s) Type	Summary of Operation	Notes
? :	Boolean, any, any	Ternary conditional operator; tests a statement and returns the value of one operand	
delete	Object, property, array element	Deletes objects, properties, and array elements	JavaScript 1.2 and higher
new	Object type	Creates an instance of any object with a constructor	
typeof	Any	Returns the type of its operand	
void	Any	Evaluates an expression and returns undefined value	
&	Integers	Calculates bitwise AND	
&=	Integers	Calculates bitwise AND, assigns new value	
|	Integers	Calculates bitwise OR	
|=	Integers	Calculates bitwise OR, assigns new value	
^	Integers	Calculates bitwise XOR	
^=	Integers	Calculates bitwise XOR, assigns new value	
~	Integers	Calculates bitwise NOT	
<<	Integers	Calculates bitwise left shift	
<<=	Integers	Calculates bitwise left shift, assigns new value	
>>	Integers	Calculates bitwise right shift	
>>=	Integers	Calculates bitwise right shift, assigns new value	
>>>	Integers	Calculates bitwise right shift with zero fill	
>>>=	Integers	Calculates bitwise right shift with zero fill, assigns new value	

Table 1-7.   Summary of Operators *(continued)*

JavaScript Operators

JavaScript has binary and unary operators, and one ternary operator. A unary operator requires only one operand, a binary requires two, and a ternary operator requires three operands.

Operands

An operand can be any "thing" in JavaScript such as a number or string, a variable, or an object.

Operator Precedence

Operators have lower and higher precedence over one another. For example, the * operator has a higher precedence than the + operator. Operator precedence declines in the order shown in Table 1-8.

High	.	[]	()								
	++	«--	-	~	!	delete	new	typeof	void		
	*	/	%								
	+	-									
	<<	>>	<<<								
	<	>	<=	=>							
	==	!=	===	!==							
	&										
	^										
	|										
	||										
	&&										
	?:										
	=	*=	/=	%=	+=	-=	<<=	>>=	>>>=	&=	^=	|=
Low	,										

Table 1-8.   Operator Precedence

Left to Right

.	[ ]	( )	*
/	%	+	–
<<	>>	>>>	<
<=	>	>=	==
!=	===	!==	&
^	|	&&	||
,			

Table 1-9.   JavaScript Operators That Associate from Left to Right

Operator Associativity

JavaScript operators associate either left to right, as shown in Table 1-9, or right to left, as shown in Table 1-10.

Right to Left

++	((--	–	~
!	delete	new	typeof
void	*	/	%
?:	*=	/=	%=
+=	–=	<<=	>>=
>>>=	&=	^=	|=

Table 1-10.   JavaScript Operators That Associate from Right to Left

Types of Operators

Arithmetic Operators

Addition (+)   The + operator is a binary operator. It adds numbers,

```
z = 3 + 4; // z is now equal to 7
```

and it concatenates strings:

```
z = "3" + "4" // z is now equal to 34
greeting = "Hel" + "lo";
// greeting is now equal to "Hello"
```

Subtraction (-)   When used as a binary operator, - subtracts numbers from one another.

```
x = 4 - 3; // x is now equal to 1
x = 3 - 4; // x is now equal to -1
```

When used as a unary operator, - converts a positive number into a negative number, and vice versa.

```
x = 6;
y = -x; // y is now equal to -6
z = -y; // z is now equal to 6
```

If - is used with non-numeric values, it will try to calculate the difference by converting them to numeric values.

Multiplication (*)   The * operator is a binary operator used to multiply two numbers together.

```
z = 2 * 3; // z is now equal to 6
```

If * is used with non-numeric values, it will try to calculate the product by converting them to numeric values.

Division (/)   The / operator is a binary operator that divides its first operand by the second.

```
z = 6 / 3; // z is now equal to 2
z = 3 / 2; // z is now equal to 1.5
```

Dividing by zero generates special values.

```
z = 3 / 0; /* z now equals POSITIVE_INFINITY or NEGATIVE_
INFINITY */
z = 0 / 0; // z now equals NaN
```

If / is used with non-numeric values, it will try to convert the values to numbers and then calculate the quotient.

Divide for Remainder (%)   The % operator is also called modulo. It returns the remainder that is left after dividing two operands.

```
z = 7 % 2; // z is now equal to 1
z = 6 % 2; // z is now equal to 0
```

If % is used with non-numeric values, it will try to calculate the remainder by converting the values to numbers.

Increment (++)   The ++ operator is a unary operator used to increment a number, or add one to it.

The ++ operator can either pre-increment or post-increment. Pre-incrementing means the number is incremented *before* other operations in the statement are executed. In the following example, x is pre-incremented.

```
x = 5;
y = ++x; // x and y are both equal to 6 now
```

When post-incrementing with ++, the number is incremented *after* other operations in the statement are executed. In the following example, x is post-incremented.

```
x = 5;
y = x++; // x is now equal to 6, y is equal to 5
```

The ++ operator will attempt to convert non-numeric values to numbers before incrementing them.

Decrement (--)   The -- operator is a unary operator used to decrement a number, or subtract one from it.

The — operator can either pre-decrement or post-decrement. Pre-decrementing means the number is decremented *before* other operations in the statement are executed. In the following example, x is pre-decremented.

```
x = 5;
y = --x; // x and y are both equal to 4 now
```

When post-decrementing with --, the number is decremented *after* other operations in the statement are executed. In the following example, x is post-decremented.

```
x = 5;
y = x--; // x is now equal to 4, y is equal to 5
```

The -- operator will attempt to convert non-numeric values to numbers before decrementing them.

String Operators

Concatenate (+)   The + operator concatenates two line strings into one.

```
greeting = "Have a " + "nice day." /*
greeting now equals "Have a nice day." */
```

Concatenate and Assign (+=)   The += operator concatenates two strings while changing the value of the first operand.

```
greeting = "Hello";
greeting += " World!"; /*
greeting now equals "Hello World!" */
```

Compare Alphabetically (>, >=, <, <=)   The >, >=, <, and <= operators compare strings according to alphabetical order.

```
x = ("a" < "b"); /* x is true because "b" is higher
in the alphabet than "a" */
x = ("ape" > "banana"); /* x is false because
"banana" is higher in the alphabet than ape */
```

Logical Operators

Logical AND (&&)   The && operator is a binary operator. &&
evaluates to true when the statements on both sides of && are
true. Non-empty strings, non-zero and positive values, and true
expressions all evaluate to true. See the following examples.

```
x = (1 && 1); // x is true
x = (0 && 1); // x is false
x = ("cat" && "dog"); // x is true
x = ("cat" && null); // x is false
```

Logical OR (||)   The || operator is a binary operator. || returns
the value of the expression on the left side of the || *if* the left-hand
value is positive, non-zero, or true. Otherwise, if the value of the
right-hand expression is positive, non-zero, or true, it returns the value
of the expression on the right side of the ||. If the value on the right
side is not true, the left-hand value is returned.

One exception to this is in Netscape Navigator 2 and 3, where || will
return simply true if the right-hand expression evaluated to true.

```
x = ("hello" || "hi"); // x is "hello"
x = (0 || "hi"); // x is "hi"
x = (-2 || 0); // x is -2
```

Logical NOT (!)   The ! operator is a unary operator. It returns
true if its operand is negative, zero, or false. Otherwise, !
returns true.

```
x = null;
y = !x; // y is true
```

Bitwise Operators

Bitwise operators treat operands as binary numbers rather than as
integers. For this reason, they aren't commonly needed.

Bitwise AND (&)   The & operator is a binary operator that will only
accept integers that can be represented as 32-bit integers. & works
by converting its two operands to binary, and then comparing them
bit by bit. The results of this comparison are applied to each bit.

```
x = 9 & 3; // x is now equal to 1
```

Bitwise OR (|) The | operator is a binary operator that will only accept integers that can be represented as 32-bit integers. | works by converting its two operands to binary, and then comparing them bit by bit. | applies the results of the comparison to each bit.

```
x = 9 | 3; // x is now equal to 11
```

Bitwise Exclusive OR (^) The ^ operator is a binary operator that will only accept integers that can be represented as 32-bit integers. After ^ converts each integer to binary, it compares each bit using an exclusive OR, which requires one bit or the other to be on, but not both. The results of the comparison are applied bit by bit.

```
x = 9 ^ 3; // x is now equal to 10
```

Bitwise NOT (~) The ~ operator is a unary operator that will only accept integers that can be represented as 32-bit integers. After ~ converts its single integer to binary, it reverses all bits in the integer.

```
x = ~9; // x is now equal to -10
```

Left Shift (<<) The << operator is a binary operator that will only accept integers that can be represented as 32-bit integers. After << converts its first operand to binary, it adds however many zeros the second operand specifies to the left of the number. Any excess bits shifted to the left are discarded.

```
x = 9 << 3; // x is now equal to 72
```

Sign-Propagating Right Shift (>>) The >> operator is a binary operator that will only accept integers that can be represented as 32-bit integers. After >> converts its first operand to binary, it adds however many zeros the second operand specifies to the right of the number. Any excess bits shifted to the right are discarded.

```
x = 9 >> 3; // x is now equal to 1
```

Zero-Fill Right Shift (>>>) The >>> operator is a binary operator that will only accept integers that can be represented as 32-bit integers. After >>> converts its first operand to binary, it adds however many zeros the second operand specifies to the right of the number. Any excess bits shifted to the right are discarded and zero bits are shifted in from the left.

```
x = 9 >>> 3; // x is now equal to 1
```

Assignment Operators

Assignment (=)   The = operator is a binary operator used simply to assign a value to a variable.

```
x = 1; // x is now equal to 1
```

Assignment and Operation   Assignment and operation operators are used for shorthand. In the following example a line of code is easily shortened using an assignment and operation operator.

```
x = x + 20; // No assignment operator usedx += 20;
// Same result with assigment operator
```

Like most shorthand conventions, assignment operators can look intimidating to new programmers. For the benefit of these programmers, Table 1-11 provides examples of shorthand operators and their equivalents.

Shorthand Operator	Example	Meaning
+=	x += 2;	x = x + 2;
-=	x -= 2;	x = x - 2;
*=	x *= 2;	x = x * 2;
/=	x /= 2;	x = x / 2;
%=	x %= 2;	x = x % 2;
<<=	x <<= 2;	x = x << 2;
>>=	x >>= 2;	x = x >> 2;
>>>=	x >>>= 2;	x = x >>> 2;
&=	x &= 2;	x = x & 2;
^=	x ^= 2;	x = x ^ 2;
|=	x |= 2;	x = x | 2;

Table 1-11.   Assignment and Operation Operators

Equality Operators

Equality (==)   The == operator tests two values for equality and returns true if the values are equal or `false` if they are not.

The == operator can be used to compare numbers, strings, and references to objects. Two numbers are equal when both have the same value.

```
x = (5 == 5.00); // x is true
x = (5 == 5.0000001); // x is false
```

Two strings are identical when they contain the same letters.

```
x = ("Hi" == "Hi"); // x is false
x = ("Hi!" == "Hi."); // x is false
x = ("Hi" == "hi"); // x is false
```

Two variables that contain references to objects will evaluate to true only if they reference the same object.

```
var myDay = new Date();
var yourDay = myDay;
x = (myDay == yourDay); // x is true
```

If two variables do not reference the same object, they won't evaluate to true when compared using ==, even if the object is identical.

```
var myDay = new Date();
var yourDay = new Date();
x = (myDay == yourDay); // x is false
```

If two operands of different types are compared with ==, the operator will try to convert the operands to the same type to compare them.

```
x = ("12" == 12); // x is true, with one exception
. . .
```

The only exception to this rule is JavaScript 1.2 in Netscape Navigator, which won't attempt any type conversion. This is only a problem when you explicitly define the language as `JavaScript1.2` in the `language` attribute of the `script` tag of your HTML document.

Finally, two `null` values test equal to each other, a `null` value tests equal to NaN and `undefined`, but two NaNs are not equal to each other. Also, NaN is not equal to `undefined`.

Inequality (!=) This `!=` operator is a unary operator that tests two values for equality and returns `true` if the two values are not equal or `false` if the two values are equal.

The `!=` operator behaves exactly opposite the `==` operator. It can be used to compare numbers, strings, and references to objects.

If two operands are numbers and are equal, `!=` returns `false`.

If two operands are strings and contain exactly the same letters, `!=` returns `false`.

When the operands are two references to objects, `!=` only returns `false` when the two references point to the same object. If they reference identical, separate objects `!=` returns `true`.

See the previous equality (==) operator for examples.

Identity (===) The `===` operator tests for equality much like the `==` operator, except `===` evaluates to `true` only if the two values are of the same variable type. See the following example:

```
x = (5 === 5); // x is true
x = ("5" === 5); // x is false
```

The identity operator is available only in JavaScript 1.3 and higher.

Non-identity (!==) The `!==` operator is the exact opposite of the `===` operator. It evaluates to true when two values are not exactly equal, and false when two values are exactly equal. See the preceding `===` operator for more information.

Comparison Operators

Greater Than (>) The `>` operator returns `true` when the first operand is greater than the second operand.

```
x = (4 > 3); // x is true
```

When two strings are compared, > will try to convert them to numbers. If the strings can't be converted to numbers, they're compared by alphabetical order.

```
x = ("4" > "3"); // x is true
x = ("dog" > "cat"); /* x is true, because "dog"
comes after "cat" in alphabetical order. */
```

Greater Than or Equal (>=)   The >= operator returns true when the first operand is greater than *or equal to* the second operand.

```
x = (4 >= 3); // x is true
x = (4 >= 4); // x is true
```

>= converts strings to numbers when it can, and otherwise uses alphabetical order. See greater than (>), earlier in the chapter, for an example.

Less Than (<)   The < operator returns true when the first operand is less than the second operand. See the following example:

```
x = 3 < 4; // x is true
```

When two strings are compared, < will try to convert them to numbers. If the strings can't be converted to numbers, they're compared by alphabetical order.

```
x = ("4" < "3"); // x is true
x = ("dog" < "cat"); /* x is false, because "dog"
comes after "cat" in alphabetical order. */
```

Less Than or Equal (<=)   The <= operator returns true when the first operand is greater than *or equal to* the second operand.

```
x = (3 <= 4); // x is true
x = (4 <= 4); // x is true
```

<= converts strings to numbers when it can, and otherwise uses alphabetical order. See less than (<),preceding, for an example.

Special Operators

Ternary Conditional Operator (? :)   The ? : operator can be used as a replacement for an if statement. Of its three operands, the first operand is an expression or variable that evaluates to `true` or `false`. If the first operand evaluates `true`, the value of the second operand is returned. If the first operand returns `false`, the value of the second operand is returned.

```
x = false;
y = (x ? "Red" : "Blue"); // y equals "Blue"
```

typeof   The unary operator `typeof` returns the type of its operand. It can be written in either of two ways,

```
typeof x;
```

or

```
typeof(x);
```

There are many different values that can be returned by the function. Table 1-12 lists a few.

NOTE: `typeof` is available in JavaScript 1.1 and higher.

Object Creation Operator (new)   The unary operator `new` takes one operand that is the name of an object type. `new` is used to create an instance of any JavaScript object that has a constructor function.

```
x = new Date(); // x is reference to a Date object
```

Value Type	Returns String
Undefined	`"undefined"`
Null	`"object"`
Boolean	`"boolean"`
Number	`"number"`
Most native JavaScript objects	`"function"`
Other native JavaScript objects	`"object"`
Object defined by user	Implementation dependent

Table 1-12.   Values Returned by `typeof`

Delete Operator (delete)   The `delete` operator takes a single operand that can be the name of an object, object property, or an element in an array. `delete` attempts to delete the operand. If it is successful, it returns `true`. If it is unsuccessful, it returns `false`.

```
x = new Date(); // x is a reference to a Date object
y = delete x; // y is true, x is undefined
```

You can also use `delete` to delete object properties, but not variables created with `var`. See the following example.

```
x = new Number();
// x is a reference to a Number object x.value1 = 42;
// creates property value1, which equals 42y = delete x.value1;
// y is true, x.value1 is undefined
```

Void Operator (void)   The operator `void` takes a single operand, which is an expression. The expression is evaluated without returning a value.

```
void(0);
```

Comma Operator (,)   The `,` operator takes two operands, both expressions. It evaluates both operands and returns the value of the second operand. It can be used as a shortcut to place multiple expressions on one line. For example, the following lines of code

```
x = 1;
y = 2;
z = 3;
```

can be condensed into one line using the comma operator:

```
x = 1, y = 2, z = 3;
```

Function Call Operator (())   The `()` operator is used to call a JavaScript function. The operator has no fixed number of operands; it's dependent on the particular function that is being called to determine the number of operands.

```
alert("Hello, World.");
history.go(-1);
```

Object Access Operator (.)   The . operator takes two operands—an object name on the left and a property or method name on the right. The . operator is used to access an object's properties and methods.

```
navigator.plugins[]
history.go()
document.URL
```

Chapter 2
Statements and Control Structures

In this chapter, we will discuss Statements and Control Structures. These are the building blocks of JavaScript. Statements define the layout of JavaScript, including expression statements, variables, functions, and so on. Control Structures make Statements more useful, by allowing you to do things conditionally, such as in if...else statements, and in loops, such as for and while loops.

Statements

Expression Statements

An expression statement assigns a value to a variable or executes a function.

```
greeting = "Welcome!"; // this expression assigns a value to
greeting
alert(greeting); // this expression executes a function
```

Compound Statements

A compound statement groups as many statements as you like into one statement block.

```
{
  url = "http://www.yahoo.com";
  document.location = url;
}
```

var

The var statement is used to explicitly define any amount of variables. The keyword var can precede any amount of variables separated by commas, optionally with initial values.

```
var x = 42; // defines one variable
var x = 42, y, dog = "poodle", win = window.name, z;
  // defines 5 variables
```

function

A function statement is used to define a function, including its arguments and body. A function can have any number of arguments separated by commas. Both the parentheses and the curly brackets are required.

```
function doubleX() {
  x *= 2;
} // this function has no arguments

function multiply(x,y) {
  var product = x * y;
  return product;
} // this function has two arguments
```

return

The return statement is used to specify what value will be returned by the function when it is executed.

```
function triple(number) {
  return number + 3;
}
```

with

The with statement is used to temporarily change the working scope. To save yourself some typing, for example, you might code the following:

```
with(document.myForm) {
   if ((name.value == "Grover") && (password.value ==
"sesame")) {
      submit();
   }
}
```

In this case, using the `with` statement saves the coder from having to type

```
document.myForm.name.value, document.myForm.
password.value, and document.myForm.submit().
```

Using abbreviations also reduces a script's file size, which results in faster download times for scripts that are embedded in web pages.

import and export

The `import` and `export` statements are available in Netscape 4 only. They work in the following manner. First, an `export` statement is used on a property inside a window or layer. Then the variable available to scripts outside that window or layer is accessed using an `import` statement.

For example, one window named `win1` can contain the following code:

```
x = 101;
export x;
```

After this code is executed, another browser window can access `x` and modify after executing an `import` statement.

```
import x;
x = 99;
```

The Empty Statement

An empty statement can be executed to do absolutely nothing. This can be represented with one semicolon, preceded by nothing. The empty statement is rarely useful, but you can use it where a statement is mandatory but you don't actually want to execute one.

```
for (count=0; count<array.length; count++;) {
  ; // this is an empty statement
}
```

try...catch

A try...catch statement can be used for error handling in
JavaScript 1.3 and above. First, try executes a statement block.
If an error occurs, a statement block in the catch statement is
executed. This doesn't cancel the execution of the code in the try
statement; it simply aborts at the moment right before erroneous
code would be executed.

```
try {
  doSomething();
} // If the execution of this code generates an error
catch (e) {
  errorOccurred(e);
} // then the Exception object e is created and this
//code is executed
```

Control Structures

Conditional

if...else

The if statement allows JavaScript to execute a statement block if
a logical condition is true. For example:

```
if (CarSize) {
// if condition is true, execute this statement block
  CarSeats = 5;
}
```

Comparison of information is another way to utilize the if statement.
Comparisons simply test variables against text strings, number
strings, boolean strings, other variables, and so on.

```
if (CarSize != "small") {
  document.write("You do not have a small car.");
}
```

The `else` statement may be used along with the `if` statement to execute a statement block, if the condition is false.

```
if (CarSize) {
  // if condition is true, execute this statement block
  CarSeats = 5;
  document.write("Your car has " + CarSeats + " seats.");
  // This displays: Your car has 5 seats.
}
else {
  // if condition is false, execute this statement block
  document.write("You do not have a car.");
}
```

You may also compare two or more things using an `if...else` statement:

```
if ((CarPrice = "low") || (CarSize = "small")) {
  CarType = 'consumer';
  document.write("You drive a " + CarType + " car.");
  // This displays: You drive a consumer car.
}
else {
  document.write("You drive a luxury car.");
}
```

The `else` statement may also be used, for comparing, as a conclusion:

```
if (CarSeats = 2) {
  CarType = 'small';
  document.write("You drive a " + CarType + " car.");
}
if ((CarSeats > 2) && (CarSeats < 5)) {
  CarType = 'medium';
  document.write("You drive a " + CarType + " car.");
}
else {
  // We have already determined that small cars have 2 seats,
  // and medium cars have more than 2 seats AND less than 5 seats.
  // This statement block concludes that all other possibilities
```

```
    // are large.
    CarType = 'large';
    document.write("You drive a " + CarType + " car.");
}
```

The if and else statements may also be nested within other if and else statements.

```
if (CarSize != "small") {
  if (CarSeats <= 4) {
    // medium cars are not small and have
    // four or fewer seats
    CarSize = 'medium';
    document.write("You drive a " + CarSize + " car.");
  }
  else {
    CarSize = 'large';
    document.write("You drive a " + CarType + " car.");
  }
}
```

else if

The else if statement may be used instead of nesting several else statements inside other if statements. More simply, else if is a coding shortcut, used to decrease the number of nested statements and shorten your code. As you can see, the following code contains quite a few nested statements:

```
if (CarSize = "small") {
  // Execute this statement block
  document.write("You drive a small car.");
}
else {
  if (CarSize = "medium") {
    // Execute this statement block
    document.write("You drive a medium car.");
  }
  else {
    if (CarSize = "large") {
      // Execute this statement block
      document.write("You drive a large car.");
    }
  }
}
```

This script may be shortened quite a bit, from 16 lines to 12. Another advantage to using the else if statement, rather than nested `else` and `if` statements, is that it makes your scripts easier for you and other developers to read.

```
if (CarSize = "small") {
  // Execute this statement block
  document.write("You drive a small car.");
}
else if (CarSize = "medium") {
  // Execute this statement block
  document.write("You drive a medium car.");
}
else if (CarSize = "large") {
  // Execute this statement block
  document.write("You drive a large car.");
}
```

switch

The `switch` statement is simply a matching and execution tool. It is used to compare an expression against various cases. If the expression matches the case, then the case's statement block is executed. The statement block for each case may end with a `break`; if omitted, the `switch` statement continues to the next case. The `switch` statement may also end with a `default` case, which will be executed if none of the other cases match the expression.

```
switch (CarSize) {
  case "small" :
    document.write("You drive a small car.");
    break;
  case "medium" :
    document.write("You drive a medium car.");
    break;
  case "large" :
    document.write("You drive a large car.");
    break;
  default :
    document.write("Your car is " + i + " sized");
```

As you can see, the preceding `switch` example is much cleaner looking than the `if` and `else` statements shown earlier in this chapter.

Loops

Loops are commands that are continually executed until a particular condition is met. Several loop statements are used with JavaScript:

for, while, do-while, and for-in. The label, break, and continue statements are used within loops, to increase functionality. Also, the for-in statement is used for object manipulation. There are several loop statements that are used with JavaScript: for, while, do-while, and for-in.

while

The while statement is used to execute the statement while a condition is true.

```
valueA = 0;
valueB = 100;
while(valueA < valueB) {
  document.write("<br>" + valueA);
  valueA++;
  }
```

This example will print the numbers 0 through 99, each on a new line. During each statement execution, valueA first prints on a new line, and then increases by 1. After the statement executes, we return to the while statement, which evaluates if valueA is less than valueB. If this is true, then the statement executes again and again until valueA is greater than valueB.

do-while

The do...while loop is very similar to the while loop. It executes a statement block while a condition is true, but the conditional testing occurs at the bottom of the loop. The do-while loop is useful for making sure a statement is executed at least once. For example:

```
valueA = 0;
valueB = 100;
do {
  document.write("<BR>" + valueB);
  valueB--;
} while (valueB != 0); // This loop will cycle 100 times
```

for

The for loop may be used for loops that are count controlled. The first line of a for statement specifies three things: a value that can be declared or stated, the condition for exiting the loop, and a statement that will be executed as the loop cycles.

```
valueA = 100;
for (valueB = 50; valueA < valueB; valueB++) {
  document.write("Current value is: " + valueB + "<br>");
}
```

for-in

The `for-in` loops are most commonly used with arrays, where the variable is automatically incremented and the loop is executed once for each element in the array.

```
for (valueX in myArray) {
  document.write("myArray Item Number:" + valueX + "<BR>");
  document.write("myArray Item: " + myArray[valueX] + "<BR>");
}
```

break and continue

The `break` statement simply causes the current loop or switch statement to exit.

```
for (valueA = 0; valueA < 10; valueA++) {
  if (valueA = 5) {
    break;
  }
}
```

The `continue` statement restarts the current loop with a new iteration.

```
valueA = 0;
valueB = 10;
for (valueA = 0; valueA < 11; valueA++) {
  if (valueA != valueB) {
    continue;
  }
  document.write("This value: " + valueA);
}
// This would only print: This value: 10
```

You may also use `continue` with a statement that has been labeled.

```
continue label;
```

label

You use label statements to identify loops within JavaScript so that you may later refer to them using break and continue. Labels aren't often useful because break and continue can also be used without a label.

```
counter:
for (valueA = 0; valueA < 10; valueA++) {
  if (test) {
    break counter;
  } else {
    continue counter;
  }
}
```

Chapter 3
Functions and Objects

Functions

Defining Functions

A function is a set of statements that performs a task. Functions may be split into three common categories: function keywords, function constructors, and function literals. Table 3-1 shows different ways to create a new function in different versions of JavaScript.

`function` Keywords

One way to define a function is to use the `function` keyword. Following the `function` keyword is the function name, which may be anything except reserved words. After the function name, in parenthesis, are optional parameters; the parameters may be words or numbers.

```
function myBox(width,length) {
  var SqInches = length * width;
  document.write("My box is " + SqInches + " square inches.<br>");
  }
```

`function` keyword	All versions of JavaScript
`Function()` constructor	JavaScript 1.1 and higher
Function literal	JavaScript 1.2 and higher

Table 3-1.   Defining Functions with Different Versions of JavaScript

`Function()` Constructors

`Function()` constructors are used to dynamically create functions. This allows you to create a function as part of an expression.

```
var myBox = new Function("length", "width", "return length*width;")
```

Function Literals

Function literals may also be called anonymous functions, since they do not have names. Function literals allow functions to be embedded in variables.

```
var myBox = function(length,width,height) { return
length*width*height; }
```

Function literals are convenient because they may be used once and then ignored by the rest of the script.

Executing Functions

In order to "activate" a function, it must be executed. To execute a function, you must type the function name, followed by parenthesis, which include optional parameters.

```
// sample function and execution
function myBox(height,width) {
  var SqInches = length*width;
  document.write("My box is " + SqInches + " square inches.<BR>");
  }
myBox(12,10,100);
// This execution displays the following line:
// My box is 12000 square inches.
```

If you specify three parameters when you define a function, you must call the function with three parameters when executing. If you do not, a JavaScript undefined error will most likely occur. If you use more than the three expected parameters, only the first three will be used by the function.

Nested Functions

Like loop statements, functions may be nested. Nested functions expand the usability and functionality of scripts.

```
// this script demonstrates the area of several boxes
function myBox(height,width,boxes) {
```

```
function addbox(num) { return (height*width)*num; }
document.write("The combined area of my boxes is " + addbox(boxes)
+ " cubic inches");
}
myBox(10,12,15);
// this will display the following line:
// The combined area of my boxes is 1800 cubic inches.
```

Manipulating Functions as Data

A powerful aspect of JavaScript is that functions may be manipulated as data. This allows JavaScript to treat functions as any data value. For instance, you can first define the function mySalary():

```
var myRate = 5.33;
function mySalary(HoursWorked) { return myRate*HoursWorked; }
```

And then you can use that function name in other variables, and it will return the proper data.

```
WeekPay = mySalary(40) // Week contains 213.2
DailyPay = mySalary(8) // Day contains 42.64
MonthlySalary = (Day * 30) // MonthlySalary contains 1279.2
YearlySalary = (Week * 52) // YearlySalary contains 11086.4
document.write("I make $" + YearlySalary + " per year");
```

Methods and Properties

Functions are a type of JavaScript object, the Function object. Because of this, they come with certain preset methods and properties.

The call Object   Each JavaScript function executes in a local scope, which is different from the global, or "scriptwide," scope. A function scope may be created by using the call object. By adding the call object to the front of the scope chain, you can access the properties of this object from the body of the function. Properties of this object include local variables, as well as parameters of the function. In addition, the call object defines the arguments property.

The arguments Property   This property refers to the arguments object. The arguments object contains two useful properties, and may also be used as an array, that holds arguments passed to the function. The arguments[] array gives you access to all of the arguments that a function is passed, even if it is passed more or fewer arguments than expected. The first function passed to the `arguments[]` array can be accessed as `arguments[0]`. The `length` property may also be used with the `arguments[]` array to determine the number of elements contained.

```
function DOB(Month, Day, Year) {
  if (!arguments[0]) {
    alert("The DOB function is missing the month of birth");
    return null;
  }
  if (!arguments[1]) {
    alert("The DOB function is missing the day of birth");
    return null;
  }
  if (!arguments[2]) {
    alert("The DOB function is missing the year of birth");
    return null;
  }
  if (arguments.length > 3) {
    alert("The DOB function passed " + arguments.length +
" arguments.");
    return null;
  }
  // Actual body of the function goes here
}
```

Navigator 4 combines the `call` object and the `arguments` object into one object. While invoking the `toString()` method of the `arguments` object of a function, calling the method returns the string `'[object Call]'`.

The two other properties of the `arguments` object are `callee` and `caller`.

The `callee` property was implemented in JavaScript 1.2. JavaScript 1.4 deprecated `callee` as a property of `Function.arguments`, and retained it as a property of a function's local `arguments` variable. The `arguments.callee` property may only be used in the body of a function. The `arguments.callee` property is used to return the function that it resides in.

```
function DisplayFunction() {
  return arguments.callee;
}
```

The preceding function will return itself:

```
function DisplayFunction() {
  return arguments.callee;
}
```

This is useful for doing something recursively.

```
var x = 0;
function NumberList(x) {
  if (x < 10) {
    document.write(x);
    arguments.callee(x+1);
  }
}
// This function will print each number
// from 0 to 9.
```

The `arguments.caller` property was introduced in JavaScript 1.1 and deprecated in JavaScript 1.3. Like the `callee` property, the `caller` property is only available in the body of a function. The `caller` property returns the name of the function from which it was called.

```
function tester() {
  return arguments.caller;
}
function trythis() {
  tester;
}
// the tester() function returns: trythis()
```

You can also use `callee` and `caller` together as `arguments.caller.callee`. This property returns the function from which it was called.

```
function tester() {
  return arguments.caller;
}
function trythis() {
  tester;
}
// the tester() function returns the entire trythis()
function.
```

length and arity   The `length` property of a function allows you to get the number of arguments that a function expects. For

3

example, you could define a `multiply()` function, and then confirm
the amount of arguments it expects with the following code:

```
function multiply(x,y,z) {
  return x * y * z;
}
document.write("multiply() takes " + multiply.length +
" arguments.");
  // writes "multiply() takes 3 arguments."
```

The `length` property of a function's `arguments` object allows
you to get the number of arguments that were actually *passed
to* a function, not the number of objects that were *expected by*
the function. You can use it to verify that the correct number
of arguments is passed to a function in order to catch an error
before one occurs.

```
function multiply(x,y,z) {
  if (arguments.length == 3) {
    return x * y * z;
  } else {
    return "Please pass exactly 3 arguments."; }
}
var n = multiply(2,2,3); // returns 12
var p = multiply(3,0); // returns "Please pass exactly 3 arguments."
```

Although `length` in both senses was introduced in JavaScript 1.1,
it will not work in several early versions of Netscape 4, unless you
specify `'JavaScript1.2'` in your `<SCRIPT>` tag explicitly.

The `arity` property of the `arguments` object is a deprecated property
that has exactly the same results as the `length` property of the
`function` object. It works in Navigator 4 only.

prototype   When a function is used as a constructor for a new
object, it has a `prototype` object. See the sections "Constructors"
and "Prototypes," later in this chapter, for more information.

Defining Function Properties   Defining your own function
properties creates a static variable that can be used only within
the function where it was defined. We can make a new function
property in the following code:

```
var calcTax.r = 4.5
function calcTax(x) {
  return x * r;
}
```

apply() and call()

The `apply()` and `call()` methods were introduced into the `function` object in JavaScript 1.3.

You can use `apply()` to execute a function as though it were a method of another object. To use the `apply()` method, you must pass it the name of an object and an array of arguments to pass to that object. `apply()` can be executed with the following syntax:

```
functionName.apply(objectName, [arg1, arg2, arg3]);
    // With the apply() method, arguments are passed in an array.
```

The `call()` method of a function does the same thing as `apply()`, but the arguments it receives for a function are simply in a comma-separated list rather than in an array. `call()` can be executed with this syntax:

```
functionName.call(objectName, arg1, arg2, arg3);
    // With the call() method, arguments are passed
       in an argument list.
```

Objects

JavaScript is an object-oriented language. There are many jobs that can't be done without objects in JavaScript, and countless others that can be streamlined using objects.

A Prototype-Based Language

JavaScript is a prototype-based language, as opposed to Java and C++, which are class-based languages. Class-based languages require a programmer to define a class fully and then define instances of that class, or objects, at runtime. An object in a class-based language contains exactly the same methods and properties as the class it represents, and new methods and properties cannot be added when the object is declared or at runtime.

A prototype-based language like JavaScript uses only objects. Each object is created from a "prototypical" object, which contains the initial methods and properties that are contained in every object. Once an object is defined, the programmer can add new methods and properties when the object is declared or at runtime. Any object can be used as a prototypical object for another object as well.

While this may take a little bit of getting used to for programmers who are accustomed to programming in more rigidly structured languages, the prototype-based structure of JavaScript provides web coders with flexibility and ease of use.

Defining Objects

Constructors

Any predefined object with a constructor function can be created with a new statement.

```
myObject = new Object; // This statement creates an empty
JavaScript object
myDate = new Date; // This statement creates a new
Date object
```

You can also define your own object constructors that can be used with a new statement later in your program. In this example, we define a Car object called myCar and set the make to Toyota and the color to red:

```
function Car(m, c) { // this function defines a constructor
for a Car object
  this.make = m;
  this.color = c;
}
var myCar = new Car("Toyota", "red");
// defines a new Car object
document.write("My " + myCar.make + " is " + myCar.color);
// This statement writes, "My Toyota is red"
```

You can also define object methods in a constructor. First define the functions that will be methods in your object, and then assign them to your object, like this:

```
function Car_increasePrice() { this.price += 100; }
function Car(m, p) { // defines the Car constructor
  this.make = m;
  this.price = p;
  this.increasePrice = Car_increasePrice;
// defines a method
}
var myCar = new Car("Toyota", 1300);
myCar.increasePrice();
document.write("My car now costs $" + myCar.price);
 // this statement writes, "My car now costs $1400"
```

Object Literals

Object literals can be used to define new objects in JavaScript 1.2 and higher. This way, you can define your own new objects without first defining an object constructor. To write an object literal, simply declare the name of your object followed by the property names and values between brackets, separated by commas.

```
var myCar = { make: "Toyota",
              price: 1300,
              color: "silver" }; // defines the myCar object
```

3

Garbage Collection

Like Java and unlike C and C++, JavaScript has automatic garbage collection, which means no destructor functions need to be defined to free up the memory consumed by JavaScript objects and properties.

However, if you'd like to explicitly clean up an object in your code, you can do so using a `delete` statement.

```
delete myObject; // explicitly deletes the object
```

The Object Superclass

In JavaScript 1.1 and higher, every JavaScript object is based on the `Object` prototype. You can declare instances of the `Object` prototype to create blank objects in your programs.

```
var myObject = new Object; // defines a blank object called myObject
```

Properties and Methods

There is one property and some methods that are built into every JavaScript function automatically because they are included in the `Object` prototype.

The `constructor` Property   This property holds a reference to the constructor method used to create an object. It can be used in a test; but when it is written as a string, it returns the full source of the `Car` function.

```
var myCar = new Car("Toyota", 1300);
if (myCar.constructor == Car) // note the word Car is not quoted as
a string
  document.write("The constructor is Car.<br>");
```

```
  // writes "The constructor is Car."
document.write(myCar.constructor);
  // writes the JavaScript code of the Car function as a string
```

The **toString()** Method
When an object's toString() method is executed, it returns a string representation of an object. By default, it returns a reference to the object from which it was called, which translates to the string "[object Object]" and isn't normally useful.

```
document.write( myCar.toString() ); // writes, "[object Object]"
```

The exception to this default behavior is in JavaScript 1.2 in Netscape 4. In this situation, toString() returns the names and values of an object's methods and properties.

```
var myCar = new Object;
myCar.make = "Toyota";
myCar.price = 1300;
document.write(myCar.toString);
  // returns "[object Object]" in almost every situation
  // returns "{make:"Toyota", price:1300}" in JavaScript 1.2 in
Netscape 4
```

Although the default behavior of toString() isn't normally useful, redefining an object's toString() method can be very practical.

```
Car.prototype.toString = function () {
  return this.make + ", $" + this.price;
}
var myCar = new Car ("Toyota", 1300);
document.write(myCar.toString()); // writes, "Toyota, $1300"
```

The **toSource()** Method
The toSource() method of an object is supported in Netscape 4 only. It returns values of an object's methods and properties.

```
myCar = new Object;
myCar.make = "Toyota";
myCar.price = 1300;
document.write(myCar.toSource);
  // returns "{make:"Toyota", price:1300}" in Netscape 4
  // generates errors in Internet Explorer
```

The **valueOf()** Method
This method returns a number, boolean, or function to represent the value of an object. Most objects don't

have such a value, so this function most often simply returns a reference to the object from which it was called.

```
var myCar = new Object;
myCar.make = "Toyota";
myCar.price = 1300;
document.write(myCar.valueOf);
```

An object's valueOf() method can also be redefined to return a more descriptive value.

```
var myCar = new Object;
myCar.make = "Toyota";
myCar.price = 1300;
myCar.prototype.valueOf = function () {

}
document.write(myCar.valueOf);
```

The watch() and unwatch() Methods   These two methods are supported in JavaScript 1.2 with Netscape 4 only.

The watch() method of any object can be used to execute a function whenever one of the object's properties changes values. For example, you could count how many times the price property of the myCar object changed during execution of your program, and save it in a variable using the following code:

```
var myCar = new Object;
myCar.price = 1300;
var price_changes = 0;
myCar.watch("price",
  function () {
    price_changes++;
  });
```

The unwatch() method is used to remove the watch from a property. To remove the watch() on the price property, for example, you can use the following code:

```
myCar.unwatch("price");
```

Accessing Object Properties as Array Elements   Object properties can also be accessed as if they were elements in an associative array. This can be done by writing the object name,

3

followed by square brackets containing the property name in quotes.

```
document.write(myCar["price"]);
```

Using Object-Oriented JavaScript

Because object-oriented programming is a complex topic, the following sections only summarize how object-oriented features work in JavaScript and do not cover the broader topic of the object-oriented paradigm.

Classes

Class definitions don't formally exist in JavaScript. Classes are defined by defining a constructor for a class. In the following example, we'll define a constructor for the Car class, which effectively creates a prototype, or superclass, called Car.

```
function Car(m, p) { // defines the Car constructor
  this.make = m;
  this.price = p;
}
```

Inheritance

JavaScript supports inheritance through prototypes. A prototype class can be defined by defining a constructor, and then any object may inherit that class. In the following example, we'll define a Car constructor and then define an instance of the object called myCar.

```
function Car(m, p) { // defines the Car constructor
  this.make = m;
  this.price = p;
}
var myCar = new Car("Toyota", 1300);
```

Prototypes

The Object prototype isn't the only prototype available in JavaScript 1.1 and higher. Any object can be used as a prototypical object for another. In the following example, we'll define a Car class, and then use it as the prototype for both myCar and yourCar. After doing this, we're able to add a new color property to each object using the prototype object.

```
function Car(m, p) { // defines the Car constructor
  this.make = m;
  this.price = p;
}
var myCar = new Car("Toyota", 1300);
var yourCar = new Car("Honda", 2000);
// Now we'll define a new "color" property for both objects
Car.prototype.color = "silver";
document.write("My Car: " + myCar.color + " - Your Car: " +
yourCar.color);
  // Writes "My Car: silver - Your Car: silver"
```

While you can use the prototype object to set new properties in objects, you can't use it to set an existing property in every object. The following code, for example, won't work:

```
function Car(m, p) { // defines the Car constructor
  this.make = m;
  this.price = p;
}
var myCar = new Car("Toyota", 1300);
var yourCar = new Car("Honda", 2000);
// Now we'll try to change the price of both objects to 100.
Car.prototype.price = 100; // won't change the price of the
Car objects
document.write("$" + myCar.price + " - $" + yourCar.price);
  // Writes $1300 - $2000
```

You can also assign properties to built-in JavaScript objects like Number and Date using the prototype object. This will work in every browser except Internet Explorer 3 and lower.

Instance Properties and Methods

When an object is declared from a class, JavaScript makes new copies of class properties and methods. These can be called Instance Properties and Methods. Accessing and changing instance properties and executing instance variables has no impact on the prototype of the object.

Static Properties and Methods

What would be called "static" or "class" properties and methods in Java and C++ are variables that belong to a class. No new copies of static variables and methods are created when new instances of a class are declared.

Class Hierarchy

Class hierarchy is not as advanced in JavaScript as it is in class-based programming languages like Java and C++. The JavaScript class hierarchy doesn't extend farther than three tiers. First, a class is defined that inherits from the Object superclass. Next, an instance of the class is declared, completing the third tier. The code of our example of the Car superclass and the myCar object is shown here.

```
function Car(m, p) { // defines the Car constructor
  this.make = m;
  this.price = p;
}
var myCar = new Car("Toyota", 1300); // myCar is on the 3rd tier
```

The class hierarchy of this code can be represented in the following diagram:

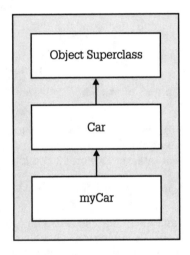

Chapter 4
Core Objects and Functions

JavaScript's core methods and objects are outlined in this chapter.
Table 4-1 summarizes these core objects and methods, and each
one is described in more detail in the following sections.

Array

The Array object provides array creation and manipulation features.
Arrays are ordered sets of values. The values that are stored in an
array are called *elements*. Elements are referred to with the name

Object/Method	Description	JavaScript Version	Notes
Array	Object-based support for arrays	1.1, ECMA-262	
Boolean	Object-based support for booleans	1.1, ECMA-262	
Date	Support for dates	1.1, ECMA-262	
Math	Contains mathematical constants and functions	1.0, ECMA-262	Static object
Number	Support for numbers, contains JavaScript-specific constant numbers	1.1, ECMA-262	
MimeType	Represents MIME types	Netscape 3 and higher only	
parseFloat()	Returns a floating-point number from a string	JavaScript 1.0, ECMA-262	Static method
parseInt()	Returns an integer from a string	JavaScript 1.0, ECMA-262	Static method
RegExp()	Provides support for regular expressions	JavaScript 1.2, ECMA-262	
String	Provides support for string manipulation and usage	JavaScript 1.0, ECMA-262	

Table 4-1.   JavaScript's Core Objects and Methods

of the array and an index number. Array index numbers are counted from zero so that, for example, the third element of an array called a would be referenced as a[2].

Although JavaScript 1.0 supported some array functionality, the Array object wasn't introduced until JavaScript 1.1. Array features were enhanced in both Netscape 4 and the ECMA-262 specification.

Table 4-2 summarizes the methods and properties in the Array object.

Method/ Property	Description	JavaScript Version	Notes
concat()	Returns an array with arguments added as new elements	1.2, ECMA-262	
join()	Returns array elements concatenated in a string	1.1, ECMA-262	
length	Provides access to the length of an array	1.1, Internet Explorer 3, ECMA-262	Enhanced in JavaScript 1.3
pop()	Removes and returns the last element from an array	Netscape 4 and higher only	
push()	Appends values to the end of an array	Netscape 4 and higher only	
reverse()	Reverses the order of elements in an array	1.1, ECMA-262	
shift()	Removes and returns the first element from an array	1.1, ECMA-262	
slice()	Returns an array that represents a portion of an array	1.2	Behaves differently in Internet Explorer 4
sort()	Sorts array elements in the specified order	1.1, ECMA-262	
splice()	Deletes a number of elements from an array, inserts values in place of deleted values	Netscape 4 and higher, ECMA-262	Enhanced in JavaScript 1.3

Table 4-2.   Methods and Properties Available in the Array Object

Method/ Property	Description	JavaScript Version	Notes
toSource()	Returns a string representing the source code of an array	1.2, ECMA-262	
toString()	Returns an array that represents a section of an array	JavaScript 1.1, ECMA-262	Netscape 4's return value differs from others
unshift()	Inserts new elements into the beginning of an array	Netscape 4 and higher only	

4

Table 4-2.   Methods and Properties Available in the Array Object *(continued)*

Creating Arrays

There are three ways to create a new array in JavaScript. The best way is usually to simply use the Array constructor, but some people prefer to use the JavaScript 1.0 method for backward compatibility, and array literals for convenience.

The Array Constructor

To create a new Array object, you can use a new statement. If you pass no arguments to the Array constructor, you'll create an empty array with a length of zero.

```
var a = new Array();
// creates an empty array with a length of 0
```

If you pass a list of values to the Array constructor, you'll create an array of those values in the same order and with a length of the number of values you passed minus one. You can pass as many values to the constructor as you like.

```
var a = new Array("Honda","Toyota","Ford");
// creates an array containing ["Honda","Toyota","Ford"]
// with a length of 3
```

If you simply pass a number to the Array constructor, you can create an empty array of that particular length.

```
var a = new Array(3);
// creates an empty array with a length of 3
```

The Array constructor is available in JavaScript 1.0 and higher.

Array Literals

Array literals can be used to define an array without a new statement. Array literals are supported in JavaScript 1.2 and later and included in the ECMA-262 specification.

```
var a = ["Honda","Toyota","Ford"];
// creates an array containing ["Honda","Toyota","Ford"]
// with a length of 3
```

Creating Arrays in JavaScript 1.0

Arrays were supported in JavaScript 1.0 using the Object prototype. You can create a JavaScript 1.0–compatible array using the following code.

```
var a = new Object();
a[0] = "Honda";
a[1] = "Toyota";
a[2] = "Ford";
// creates an array containing ["Honda","Toyota","Ford"]
```

An array defined in this way has no length property. Because it is not an actual Array object, it doesn't support Array methods and properties.

Array Methods and Properties

Following are descriptions of the methods and properties available in the Array object, to date.

concat()

The concat() method takes as many arguments as you like, concatenates them with an Array object, and returns a new Array.

concat() is available in JavaScript 1.2 and higher, and was included in the ECMA-262 specification.

```
var a = new Array("Honda","Toyota","Ford");
// creates an array, a, containing ["Honda","Toyota","Ford"]
var b = a.concat("Mazda","BMW");
// creates an array, b, containing ["Honda",
   "Toyota","Ford","Mazda","BMW"]
```

join()

The join() method returns an array's elements concatenated in a string. You can pass join() an optional argument, which is a string by which it will separate each value. If you don't pass an argument to join(), it will automatically use commas to separate each value.

join() is available in JavaScript 1.1 and higher, and was included in the ECMA-262 specification.

```
var a = new Array("Honda","Toyota","Ford");
// creates an array, a, containing ["Honda","Toyota","Ford"]
var s = a.join();
// s equals "Honda,Toyota,Ford"
var s = a.join("; ");
// s equals "Honda; Toyota; Ford"
```

length

The length attribute returns the number of elements in an Array object.

length is available in JavaScript 1.1 and higher and was included in the ECMA-262 specification. In JavaScript 1.3 and ECMA-262, length must be a positive 32-bit integer with a value less than 2^{32}.

```
var a = new Array("Honda","Toyota","Ford");
// creates an array, a, containing ["Honda","Toyota","Ford"]
// var i = a.length; // i equals 3
```

The length attribute is readable and writable. Setting the value of length to a smaller value is a good technique for deleting array elements from the end of an array. pop() and slice() can be used to do this also.

```
a.length = 2;
// a (from the previous code listing) now equals ["Honda",
// "Toyota"]
```

The length attribute is often used in a for loop to process every element in an array.

```
var numbers = new Array(1,2,3);
// creates a new array, numbers, containing [1,2,3] with a
// length of 3
for (var i=0; i<numbers.length; i++) { numbers[i]++; }
// increments each item in numbers. numbers now contains [2,3,4]
```

pop()

The pop() method deletes the last element of an array and decrements the length of the array. It takes no arguments and returns the value of the deleted element.

pop() is available in Netscape 4 and higher only.

```
var a = new Array("Honda","Toyota","Ford");
// creates an array, a, containing ["Honda","Toyota","Ford"]
// a.length equals 3
var x = a.pop()
// the array, a, now contains ["Honda","Toyota"] and its length
// is 2
// x equals "Ford"
```

push()

The push() method adds new elements onto the end of an existing Array object. It takes as many arguments as you like, which are values to be added to the array. push() returns the new length of the array.

push() is available in Netscape 4 and higher only.

```
var a = new Array("Honda","Toyota","Ford");
// creates an array, a, containing ["Honda","Toyota","Ford"]
// a.length equals 3
var x = a.push("Mazda","BMW");
// the array, a, now contains ["Honda",
// "Toyota","Ford","Mazda","BMW"]
// x and a.length both equal 5
```

The concat() method can also be used to add new values to the end of an array.

reverse()

The reverse() method reverses the order of array elements in an Array object. It takes no arguments and returns a reference to the array.

reverse() is available in JavaScript 1.1 and was included in the ECMA-262 specification.

```
var a = new Array("Honda","Toyota","Ford");
// creates an array, a, containing ["Honda","Toyota","Ford"]
var x = a.reverse();
// a new contains ["Ford","Toyota","Honda"]
// x contains a reference to Array a
```

shift()

The shift() method deletes the first element of an Array object, moves each element down to the previous place in the array, and shortens the length by one. It doesn't take any arguments and returns the deleted element.

shift() is available in Netscape 4 and higher only.

```
var a = new Array("Honda","Toyota","Ford");
// creates an array, a, containing ["Honda","Toyota","Ford"]
// a.length equals 3
var x = a.shift();
// a now contains ["Toyota","Ford"] and a.length equals 2
// x equals "Honda"
```

This can also be done using the slice() method.

slice()

The slice() method extracts a portion of an Array object and returns a new Array object. It takes two arguments. The first argument is an index at which to start selecting the slice. If this number is negative, it indicates how many elements from the end of the array to begin slicing.

The second argument is optional. It specifies the array index immediately after the last array element to be selected for the slice. If this argument isn't given, the slice will end at the end of the array. If the number points to an index that's beyond the end of the array, the selection will stop at the end of the array anyway. If the number is negative, it indicates how many array elements before the end of the array to end.

The slice() method is available in JavaScript 1.2 and later. In Internet Explorer 4 and 5, the first argument can't be a negative number.

```
var numbers = new Array(1,2,3,4,5,6);
// creates a new array, numbers, containing [1,2,3,4,5,6]
var numbers2 = numbers.slice(0,3); // slice from the beginning
  to index 2
// numbers2 contains [1,2,3]
// numbers still contains [1,2,3,4,5,6]
var numbers3 = numbers.slice(2); // slice from index 2 to the end
// numbers3 contains [3,4,5,6]
// numbers still contains [1,2,3,4,5,6]
var numbers4 = numbers.slice(2,-1); // slice from index 2 to index 4
```

4

```
// numbers4 contains [3,4,5]
// numbers still contains [1,2,3,4,5,6]
```

sort()

The sort() method sorts the elements in an Array object either numerically, alphabetically, or according to your specifications. It takes an optional argument, which is a user-defined method defining how the array items should be sorted. It returns a reference to the sorted array.

The single function that can be used as an argument must receive two arguments and return a negative number, a zero, or a positive number. If the first argument should be sorted as less than the second, the function should return a negative number. If the first argument should be sorted as greater than the second, the function should return a positive number. If the two values should be sorted as equal, the function should return a zero.

The sort() method is available in JavaScript 1.1 and later and is included in the ECMA-262 specification.

The following example sorts an array in ascending alphabetical order without using a sorting function.

```
var a = new Array("Honda","Toyota","Ford");
// creates an array, a, containing ["Honda","Toyota","Ford"]
var x = a.sort(); // a now contains ["Ford","Honda","Toyota"]
// x contains a reference to Array a
```

In the next example, a sorting function is used to sort the elements into descending order.

```
function dSort(a,b) {
// defines a function to sort in reverse order
  if (a < b) { return 1; }
  else if (a > b) { return -1; }
  if (a == b) { return 0; }
}
var a = new Array("Honda","Toyota","Ford");
// creates an array, a, containing ["Honda","Toyota","Ford"]
var x = a.sort(dSort);
// a now contains ["Toyota","Honda","Ford"]
// x contains a reference to Array a
```

splice()

The splice() method deletes a number of array elements from an Array object and replaces them with a list of values. splice() takes at least one argument, which is the index from which to start deleting array elements. The second argument is optional. This is the number of array elements to delete after the starting index. If this argument is left out, all array elements after the starting index specified in the first argument will be deleted.

The third and following arguments are also optional. These are the values to insert into the array, starting at the starting index specified in the first argument. Any other elements in the array that are not marked for deletion will be moved to accommodate any number of new values.

The `splice()` method is supported in Netscape 4 and higher, and was included in the third edition of the ECMA-262 specification. In Netscape's implementation of JavaScript 1.2, `splice()` returns nothing. In Netscape's JavaScript 1.3, `splice()` returns an array of the elements that were removed from the array.

```
var numbers = new Array(1,2,3,4,5,6);
// creates a new array, numbers, containing [1,2,3,4,5,6]
var x = numbers.splice(2,2,"a","b","c","d");
// numbers now contains [1,2,"a","b","c","d",5,6]
// x is an array containing [3,4] in JavaScript 1.3
// and higher (Netscape)
```

toString()

The `toString()` method returns a string representation of an Array object. `toString()` takes no arguments. Although `toString()` is executed automatically when an array is treated like a string, it can also be executed explicitly.

The `toString()` method is available in JavaScript 1.1 and higher, and was included in the ECMA-262 specification. In Netscape, when `toString()` is executed in <script> tags where the language attribute is set to `JavaScript 1.2`, the `toString()` method returns an array literal, between brackets.

```
var a = new Array("Honda","Toyota","Ford");
// creates an array, a, containing ["Honda",
// "Toyota","Ford"]
document.write(a);
// writes "Honda,Toyota,Ford"
document.write(a.toString());
// writes "Honda,Toyota,Ford"
```

This can also be accomplished using the `join()` function.

toSource()

The `toSource()` method returns an array literal representing an Array object. An array literal can be used in JavaScript 1.2 and higher to create a new array.

`toSource()` is supported in Netscape 4 and higher.

```
var a = new Array("Honda","Toyota","Ford");
// creates an array, a, containing ["Honda","Toyota","Ford"]
var s = a.toString();
// s equals '["Honda", "Toyota", "Ford"]'
```

unshift()

The `unshift()` method inserts a list of values onto the beginning of an Array object. It doesn't take any arguments and returns the new `length` of the array.

`unshift()` is available in Netscape 4 and higher only.

```
var a = new Array("Honda","Toyota","Ford");
// creates an array, a, containing ["Honda","Toyota","Ford"]
// a.length equals 3
var x = a.unshift("Mazda");
// a now contains ["Mazda","Honda","Toyota","Ford"] and a.
// length equals 4
// x equals 4
```

This can also be done using the `concat()` method.

Multidimensional Arrays

JavaScript doesn't support multidimensional arrays, but it supports arrays of arrays that you can use to simulate multidimensional arrays.

In the following example, we can create a pseudo-multidimensional array to store different categories of fictional employees.

```
var employees = new Array(3);
// creates the empty employees array now load employees with arrays
employees[0] = new Array("Julie","Joe","Richard","Emma");
employees[1] = new Array("Ann","Chandra","Eddy");
employees[2] = new Array("Mark","Rhonda","Paulina");
// access the values stored
document.write(employees[0][3]);
// writes "Emma"
document.write(employees[2][1]);
// writes "Rhonda"
// access an array within employees
document.write(employees[1]);
// writes "Ann,Chandra,Eddy"
```

Boolean

The Boolean object provides support for boolean, or true/false, values. Boolean is a fundamental data type in JavaScript. Boolean objects are available in JavaScript 1.1 and later, and were included in the ECMA-262 specification. A single method is available in the Boolean object:

Method	Description	JavaScript Version	Notes
toString()	Returns true or false	1.1	Doesn't need to be called explicitly

4

Creating Boolean Objects and Values

Boolean objects can be created either explicitly or implicitly.

The Boolean Constructor

Although it isn't necessary to explicitly create a Boolean object, one can be created using a new statement. The Boolean constructor takes one argument, which can be any value. Except for the special values true and false, the value will be determined true or false depending on its value. Values that are zero, an empty string, NaN, null, or undefined are all converted to false. Values that are non-zero are converted to true.

The following Boolean objects will evaluate to false:

```
var b = new Boolean(0);
var b = new Boolean(false);
var b = new Boolean(null);
var b = new Boolean(NaN);
var b = new Boolean(undefined);
var b = new Boolean("");
```

The following Boolean objects will evaluate to `true`:

```
var b = new Boolean(true);
var b = new Boolean("false");
var b = new Boolean(42);
var b = new Boolean(-42);
var b = new Boolean("The quick brown fox ...");
```

Additionally, you can use the Boolean constructor without a `new` statement to simply evaluate a value and return `true` or `false`.

```
var boolean_test = Boolean(42); // boolean_test equals true
var boolean_test = Boolean(""); // boolean_test equals false
```

Creating a Boolean Implicitly

You don't need to create a Boolean object explicitly to have access to its properties and methods. Creating a primitive Boolean value can be done like this:

```
var b = false; // sets b to false or ...
var b = true; // sets b to true
```

Boolean Methods

The Boolean object has a single method, `toString()`. Following is a description of the `toString()` method.

`toString()`

The `toString()` method returns the strings "true" or "false" depending on the value of a Boolean object. It's not normally necessary to call `toString()` explicitly because it is called automatically when a Boolean object is treated like a string.

`toString()` is available in JavaScript 1.1 and later, and was included in the ECMA-262 specification.

```
var b = new Boolean(42);
// creates a Boolean object, b,
   set to true
var s = new String(b.toString());
// sets s to "true"
document.write(b.toString());
// explicitly calls
   toString(), writes "true"
document.write(b);
// implicitly calls toString(),
   write "true"
```

Date

The Date object allows you to use and manipulate dates and times. It's available in JavaScript 1.0 and later, and some features are enhanced in JavaScript 1.1 and 1.2. The Date object is included in the ECMA-262 specification.

JavaScript represents dates internally in *millisecond format*, which is the number of milliseconds between a given date and midnight on January 1, 1970 GMT (Greenwich Mean Time).

4

Table 4-3 summarizes the methods in the Date object.

Method	Description	JavaScript Version	Notes
getDate()	Accesses the day of the month of a Date object	1.0, ECMA-262	
getDay()	Accesses the day of the week of a Date object	1.0, ECMA-262	
getFullYear()	Accesses the four-digit year of a Date object	1.2, ECMA-262	
getHours()	Accesses the hour of a Date object	1.0, ECMA-262	
getMilliseconds()	Accesses milliseconds of a Date object	1.2, ECMA-262	
getMinutes()	Accesses the minutes of a Date object	1.0, ECMA-262	
getMonth()	Accesses the month of a Date object	1.0, ECMA-262	
getSeconds()	Accesses the seconds of a Date object	1.0, ECMA-262	

Table 4-3.   Methods Available in the Date Object

Method	Description	JavaScript Version	Notes
getTime()	Accesses the date of a Date object in millisecond format	1.0, ECMA-262	
getTimezoneOffset()	Accesses the offset in hours between local time and GMT	1.2, ECMA-262	
getUTCDate()	Accesses the day of the month of a Date object in UTC	1.2, ECMA-262	
getUTCDay()	Accesses the day of the week of a Date object in UTC	1.2, ECMA-262	
getUTCFullYear()	Accesses the four-digit year of a Date object in UTC	1.2, ECMA-262	
getUTCHours()	Accesses the hour of a Date object in UTC	1.2, ECMA-262	
getUTCMilliseconds()	Accesses the milliseconds of a Date object in UTC	1.2, ECMA-262	
getUTCMinutes()	Accesses the minutes of a Date object in UTC	1.2, ECMA-262	
getUTCMonth()	Accesses the month of a Date object in UTC	1.2, ECMA-262	
getUTCSeconds()	Accesses the seconds of a Date object in UTC	1.2, ECMA-262	

Table 4-3.   Methods Available in the Date Object *(continued)*

Method	Description	JavaScript Version	Notes
getYear()	Accesses the two-digit year of a Date object	1.0, ECMA-262	Can cause millennium bugs in code; deprecated in JavaScript 1.2
parse()	Returns a date in millisecond format	1.0, ECMA-262	Static method
setDate()	Sets the day of the month of a Date object	1.0, ECMA-262	Enhanced in JavaScript 1.2
setFullYear()	Sets the four-digit year of a Date object	1.2, ECMA-262	
setHours()	Sets the hour of a Date object	1.0, ECMA-262	Enhanced in JavaScript 1.2
setMilliseconds()	Sets the milliseconds of a Date object	1.2, ECMA-262	
setMinutes()	Sets the minutes of a Date object	1.0, ECMA-262	Enhanced in JavaScript 1.2
setMonth()	Sets the month of a Date object	1.0, ECMA-262	Enhanced in JavaScript 1.2
setSeconds()	Sets the seconds of a Date object	1.0, ECMA-262	Enhanced in JavaScript 1.2
setTime()	Sets a Date object's date using millisecond format	1.0, ECMA-262	
setUTCDate()	Sets the day of the month of a Date object in UTC	1.2, ECMA-262	
setUTCFullYear()	Sets the four-digit year of a Date object in UTC	1.2, ECMA-262	
setUTCHours	Sets the hours of a Date object in UTC	1.2, ECMA-262	

Table 4-3.   Methods Available in the Date Object *(continued)*

Method	Description	JavaScript Version	Notes
setUTCMilliseconds()	Sets the milliseconds of a Date object in UTC	1.2, ECMA-262	
setUTCMinutes()	Sets the minutes of a Date object in UTC	1.2, ECMA-262	
setUTCMonth()	Sets the month of a Date object in UTC	1.2, ECMA-262	
setUTCSeconds()	Sets the seconds of a Date object in UTC	1.2, ECMA-262	
setYear()	Sets the year of a Date object	1.0, ECMA-262	Deprecated in JavaScript 1.2
toGMTString()	Returns a string representation of the Date object in GMT	1.0, ECMA-262	Deprecated in JavaScript 1.2; inconsistent between IE and Netscape
toLocaleString()	Returns a string representation of the Date object in local time	1.0, ECMA-262	
toString()	Returns a string representation of the Date object	1.1, ECMA-262	
toUTCString()	Returns a string representation of the Date object in UTC	1.2, ECMA-262	Inconsistent between IE and Netscape
valueOf()	Returns the date in millisecond format	1.1, ECMA-262	
UTC()	Returns a date in millisecond format based on date parameters	1.0, ECMA-262	Enhanced in JavaScript 1.2

Table 4-3.   Methods Available in the Date Object *(continued)*

The Date Constructor

To create a new Date object, you can use a `new` statement. If you pass no arguments to `Date()`, you'll create a Date object set to the current date and time.

```
var today = new Date();
// today is set to the current date and time
```

You can also pass a date to the Date constructor to set your new Date object to a specific date and time.

You can create a new Date object set to Sunday, July 1, 2001, 12:00:00 A.M. by passing a date specification to the Date constructor. (See "Arguments," later in this section.)

```
var myDate = new Date(2001,06,01,0,0,0,0);
// Creates a new date: 12:00:00 AM on Sunday, July 1st, 2001
```

The *hours, minutes, seconds,* and *milliseconds* arguments are optional. You can leave them out to create the same date.

```
var myDate = new Date(2001,06,01);
// Creates a new date: 12:00:00 AM on Sunday, July 1st, 2001
```

Or you can simply pass one argument, *milliseconds*, to create a date relevant to midnight on January 1, 1970 GMT.

```
var myDate = new Date(3000);
// Creates a new date: 12:00:03 AM on Thursday, January 1st, 1970
```

Arguments

Table 4-4 lists the arguments that can be passed to the Date constructor. Arguments are passed to `Date()` in this order: *year, month, day, hours, minutes, seconds, milliseconds.*

In JavaScript 1.0 and 1.1, *milliseconds* are ignored by the Date constructor.

Argument	Description	Example
year	When *year* is a four-digit date, sets the date exactly. A two-digit date sets the date to the sum of 1900 and *year*.	2001 equals 2001 01 equals 1901
month	The *month* is an integer from 0 to 11.	0 equals January 11 equals December
day	The *day* is an integer from 1 to 31.	15 equals the 15th 0 equals the 31st of the previous month.
hour	The *hour* is an integer from 0 to 23. This argument is optional.	0 equals 12:00 A.M. 14 equals 2:00 P.M. or 14:00
minute	The *minute* is an integer from 0 to 59. This argument is optional.	45 equals 45 minutes past the hour
second	The *second* is an integer from 0 to 59. This argument is optional.	45 equals 45 seconds past the minute
millisecond	The *millisecond* should be an integer from 0 to 999. Passing *millisecond* alone to the Date constructor causes the date to be set to midnight, January 1, 1970 GMT plus the number of *millisecond* specified. The *millisecond* is optional and can only be used in JavaScript 1.2 and higher. In other versions of JavaScript, *millisecond* is ignored.	300 equals 0.3 seconds 3000 equals 3 seconds Date(3000) sets the date to Thursday, January 1, 12:00:03 A.M., 1970 GMT

Table 4-4.   Arguments That Can Be Passed to the Date Constructor

Date Methods

Following are descriptions of the methods available in the Date object to date.

getDate()
The getDate() method returns the day of the month of a Date object. This will be an integer between 1 and 31.

`getDate()` is available in JavaScript 1.0 and later.

```
var d = new Date(2001,11,25); // sets the date to
   December 25th, 2001
var day = d.getDate(); // day equals 25.
```

getDay()

The `getDay()` method returns the day of the week of a Date object. This will be an integer between 0 and 6, where 0 equals Sunday and 6 equals Saturday.

`getDay()` is available in JavaScript 1.0 and later.

```
var d = new Date(2001,11,25); // sets the date to
   December 25th, 2001
var day = d.getDay(); // day equals 2, for Tuesday.
```

getFullYear()

The `getFullYear()` method returns the four-digit year of a Date object, expressed in the local time of the system that executes the code.

`getFullYear()` is available in JavaScript 1.2 and later.

```
var d = new Date(2001,11,25); // sets the date to
   December 25th, 2001
var year = d.getFullYear(); // year equals 2001
```

getHours()

The `getHours()` method returns the hour of a Date object—an integer between 0 and 23.

`getHours()` is available in JavaScript 1.0 and later.

```
var d = new Date(2001,11,25,6,30,0);
// d is set to December 25th, 2001, 6:30AM
var hour = d.getHours(); // hour equals 6
```

getMilliseconds()

The `getMilliseconds()` method returns the milliseconds of a Date object.

`getMilliseconds()` is available in JavaScript 1.2 and later.

```
var d = new Date(2001,11,25,6,30,0,20);
// d is set to December 25th, 2001, 6:30:00:02AM
var ms = d.getMilliseconds;
// ms equals 20.
```

getMinutes()

The getMinutes() method returns the minutes of a Date object.

getMinutes() is available in JavaScript 1.0 and later.

```
var d = new Date(2001,11,25,6,30,0,20);
// d is set to December 25th, 2001, 6:30:00:02AM
var min = d.getMinutes;
// min equals 30.
```

getMonth()

The getMonth() method returns the month of a Date object—an integer between 0, for January, and 11, for December.

getMonth() is available in JavaScript 1.0 and later.

```
var d = new Date(2001,11,25);
// sets d to December 25th, 2001
var month = d.getMonth();
// month equals 11, for December.
```

getSeconds()

The getSeconds() method returns the seconds of a Date object—an integer between 0 and 59.

getSeconds() is available in JavaScript 1.0 and later.

```
var d = new Date(2001,11,25,6,30,10,10);
// d is set to Dec 25th, 2001, 6:30:10:02AM
var sec = d.getSeconds();
// sec equals 10
```

getTime()

The getTime() method returns a date in millisecond format. This is the number of milliseconds between the date of a Date object and midnight, January 1, 1970 GMT. getTime() behaves identically to valueOf().

A millisecond representation of a date can be used to create a new Date object.

getTime() is available in JavaScript 1.0 and later.

```
var d = new Date(2001,11,25);
// sets d to December 25th, 2001
var gTime = d.getTime();
// gTime equals 1009256400000
```

getTimeZoneOffset()

The getTimeZoneOffset() method returns the difference, in minutes, between Greenwich Mean Time (GMT) and the local time of the computer where the code is executed.

getTimeZoneOffset() is available in JavaScript 1.0 and higher.

```
var d = new Date();
var o = d.getTimeZoneOffset;
// When executed in EST, o equals 300. In PST, o equals 480.
```

4

getUTCDate()

The getUTCDate() method returns the day of the month in universal time (UTC). UTC is basically the same as GMT. The day of the month is an integer between 1 and 31.

getUTCDate() is available in JavaScript 1.2 and later.

```
var d = new Date(2001,11,25);
// sets d to December 25th, 2001, 12:00 AM local time (by default)
var uDate = d.getUTCDate();
// uDate equals 25
```

getUTCDay()

The getUTCDay() method returns the day of the week in universal time (UTC). UTC is basically the same as GMT. The day of the month is an integer between 0 and 6.

getUTCDay() is available in JavaScript 1.2 and higher.

```
var d = new Date(2001,11,25);
// sets d to December 25th, 2001, 12:00 AM local time (by default)
var uDay = d.getUTCDay();
// uDay equals 2, for Tuesday.
```

getUTCFullYear()

The getFullYear() method returns the four-digit year of a Date object, expressed in universal time (UTC). UTC is basically the same as GMT.

getUTCFullYear() is available in JavaScript 1.2 and later.

```
var d = new Date(2001,11,25);
// sets d to December 25th, 2001, 12:00 AM local time (by default)
var uYear = d.getUTCFullYear();
// uYear equals 2001
```

getUTCHours()

The getUTCHours() method returns the hour of a Date object—an integer between 0 and 23, as expressed in universal time (UTC). UTC is basically the same as GMT.

getUTChours() is available in JavaScript 1.2 and later.

```
var d = new Date(2001,11,25,6,30,0);
// d is set to December 25th, 2001, 6:30AM
var uHour = d.getUTCHours();
// uHour equals 11 when executed in EST.
```

getUTCMilliseconds()

The getUTCMilliseconds() method returns the milliseconds in a Date object in universal time (UTC). UTC is basically the same as GMT.

getUTCMilliseconds() is available in JavaScript 1.2 and later.

```
var d = new Date(2001,11,25,6,30,0,20);
// d is set to December 25th, 2001, 6:30:00:02AM
var uMS = d.getUTCMilliseconds;
// uMS equals 20.
```

getUTCMinutes()

The getUTCMinutes() method returns the minutes of a Date object in universal time (UTC). UTC is basically the same as GMT.

getUTCMinutes() is available in JavaScript 1.2 and later.

```
var d = new Date(2001,11,25,6,30,0,20);
// d is set to December 25th, 2001, 6:30:00:02AM
var uMin = d.getMinutes;
// uMin equals 30.
```

getUTCMonth()

The getUTCMonth() method returns the month of a Date object—an integer between 0, for January, and 11, for December— expressed in universal time (UTC). UTC is basically the same as GMT.

getUTCMonth() is available in JavaScript 1.2 and later.

```
var d = new Date(2001,11,25);
// sets d to December 25th, 2001
var uMonth = d.getMonth();
// uMonth equals 11, for December.
```

getUTCSeconds()

The getUTCSeconds() method returns the day of the week in universal time (UTC). UTC is basically the same as GMT. The day of the month is an integer between 0 and 6.

getUTCSeconds() is available in JavaScript 1.2 and higher.

```
var d = new Date(2001,11,25,6,30,10,10);
// d is set to Dec 25th, 2001, 6:30:10:02AM
var sec = d.getUTCSeconds();
// sec equals 10
```

4

getYear()

The getYear() method was designed to return the year in two-digit format, but it doesn't always work that way.

In Netscape 2 and 3, getYear() returns the date in two-digit format if the date is January 1, 1900 or later, and prior to January 1, 2000. Otherwise, getYear() will return the year in four-digit format.

Internet Explorer browsers versions 4 and higher return the standard four-digit year.

Netscape browsers versions 4 and higher, and older Internet browsers, always return a date that is the difference between the set year and 1900. For example, Internet Explorer will return 95 for dates in the year 1995, and 102 for dates in the year 2002.

Netscape 4's implementation of the getYear() method behaves the same way as Internet Explorer 3's implementation.

The inconsistency between the ways this method works in different browsers can cause bugs in your code if you don't account for them carefully. I suggest using JavaScript 1.2's getFullYear() method instead, to get a four-digit year.

The getYear() method is available in JavaScript 1.0 and 1.1, and was deprecated in JavaScript 1.2 in favor of getFullYear().

```
var d = new Date(2001,11,25);
// sets d to December 25th, 2001
var y = d.getYear();
// y equals 2001 in Netscape 2, 3, and 6 and in IE 4 and higher.
// In Netscape 4 and IE 3, y equals 101.
```

parse()

The Date.parse() method will parse a string containing a date and time and returns the date in millisecond format. Here's an example of a suitable argument for Date.parse():

```
Tue, 25 Dec 2001 05:00:00 UTC
```

This is the kind of string that is created by executing Date.toGMTString(). Once a millisecond representation of a date is generated, it can be used to create a new Date object.

Date.parse() is available in JavaScript 1.0 and later.

```
var d = new Date(2001,11,25);
// sets d to December 25th, 2001
var date = d.toGMTString();
// date equals "Tue, 25 Dec 2001 05:00:00 UTC"
var i = Date.parse(date);
// i equals 1009256400000
var d2 = new Date(i);
// d2 is set to December 25th, 2001
```

Note that Date.parse() is a static method, which means it can only be executed form the Date superclass and not from instances of Date. In the preceding code, for example, I can't execute d.parse(), only Date.parse().

setDate()

The setDate() method sets the day of the month of a Date object. It receives one argument, an integer between 1 and 31.

In JavaScript 1.2 and higher, this method returns the new date in millisecond format. In JavaScript 1.0 and 1.1, it returns nothing.

setDate() is available in JavaScript 1.0 and higher.

```
var d = new Date(2001,11,25);
// sets d to December 25th, 2001
var i = d.setDate(26);
// the day of the month is now 26
// i equals 1009342800000 in JavaScript 1.2 and higher
```

setFullYear()

The setFullYear() method sets the four-digit year of a Date object. It takes one argument, a four-digit integer, and returns the new date in millisecond format. `setFullYear()` is available in JavaScript 1.2 and later.

```
var d = new Date(2001,11,25);
// sets d to December 25th, 2001
var i = d.setFullYear(2002);
// the year is now set to 2002 and i equals 1040792400000
```

setHours()

The `setHours()` method sets the hour of the day of a Date object. It takes one argument, an integer from 0, for midnight, to 23, for 11:00 p.m.

In JavaScript 1.2 and higher, `setHours()` returns the new date in millisecond format. In JavaScript 1.0 and 1.1, `setHours()` returns nothing.

`setHours()` is available in JavaScript 1.0 and later.

```
var d = new Date(2001,11,25);
// sets d to December 25th, 2001, 12:00:00 AM by default
var i = d.setHours(6);
// the time of d is now set to 6:00:00 AM
// i equals 1009278000000 in JavaScript 1.2 and higher
```

setMilliseconds()

The `setMilliseconds()` method sets the number of milliseconds of the time in a Date object. It takes one argument, an integer that should be between 0 and 999. `setMilliseconds()` returns the adjusted date in millisecond format.

`setMilliseconds()` is available in JavaScript 1.2 and higher.

```
var d = new Date(2001,11,25);
// sets d to December 25th, 2001, 12:00:00:00 AM by default
var i = d.setMilliseconds(500);
// the time of d is now set to 12:00:00:50 AM and i equals
// 1009256400500
```

setMinutes()

The `setMinutes()` method sets the minutes of the time in a Date object. It takes one argument, which should be an integer between 1 and 31.

In JavaScript 1.2, `setMinutes()` returns the new date in millisecond format. In JavaScript 1.0 and 1.1, `setMinutes()` returns nothing.

`setMinutes()` is available in JavaScript 1.0 and later.

```
var d = new Date(2001,11,25);
// sets d to December 25th, 2001, 12:00:00:00 AM by default
var i = d.setMinutes(30);
// the time of d is now set to 12:30:00:00 AM and i equals
// 1009258200000
```

setMonth()

The `setMonth()` method sets the month of a Date object. It is passed one argument, which is an integer from 0, for January, to 11, for December.

In JavaScript 1.2 and higher, `setMonth()` returns the new date in millisecond format. In JavaScript 1.0 and 1.1, `setMonth()` returns nothing.

`setMonth()` is available in JavaScript 1.0 and later.

```
var d = new Date(2001,11,25);
// sets d to December 25th, 2001
var i = d.setMonth(0);
// d is now set to January 25th, 2001
// i equals 980398800000 in JavaScript 1.2 and higher
```

setSeconds()

The `setSeconds()` method sets the number of seconds in the time of a Date object. It takes one argument, an integer that should be between 0 and 59.

In JavaScript 1.2 and higher, `setSeconds()` returns the new date in millisecond format. In JavaScript 1.0 and 1.1, `setSeconds()` returns nothing.

`setSeconds()` is available in JavaScript 1.0 and higher.

```
var d = new Date(2001,11,25);
// sets d to December 25th, 2001, 12:00:00:00 AM by default
var i = d.setSeconds(30);
// the time of d is now set to 12:00:30:00 AM
// i equals 1009256430000 in JavaScript 1.2 and higher
```

setTime()

The `setTime()` method sets the date of a Date object. This method takes one argument, a date in millisecond format. A date in millisecond format can be generated using the `Date.parse()` or the `getDate()` method.

`setTime()` is available in JavaScript 1.0 and later.

```
var d = new Date(2001,11,25); // d is set to December 25th, 2001
var i = Date.parse(d.toGMTString());
// i equals d in millisecond format
var d2 = new Date();
// d2 is set to the current date, by default
d2.setTime(i);
// d2 is set to December 25th, 2001
```

setUTCDate()

The `setUTCDate()` method sets the day of the month of a Date object in universal time (UTC). UTC is basically the same as GMT. `setUTCDate()` takes one argument, an integer between 1 and 31, and returns the new date in millisecond format.

`setUTCDate()` is available in JavaScript 1.2 and later.

```
var d = new Date(2001,11,25);
// sets d to December 25th, 2001
var i = d.setUTCDate(26);
// the day of the month is now 26, i equals 1009342800000
```

setUTCFullYear()

The `setUTCFullYear()` method sets the four-digit year of a Date object in universal time (UTC). UTC is basically the same as GMT. It receives one argument, a four-digit integer, and returns a millisecond representation of the new date.

`setUTCFullYear()` is available in JavaScript 1.2 and later.

```
var d = new Date(2001,11,25); // sets d to December 25th, 2001
var i = d.setUTCFullYear(2002);
// the year is now set to 2002 and i equals 1040792400000
```

setUTCHours()

The `setUTCHours()` method sets the hour of a day of a Date object in universal time (UTC). UTC is basically the same as GMT. It takes one argument, an integer from 0, for midnight, to 23, for 11:00 P.M., and returns the new date in millisecond format.

`setUTCHours()` is available in JavaScript 1.2 and later.

```
var d = new Date(2001,11,25);
// sets d to December 25th, 2001, 12:00:00 AM by default
var i = d.setUTCHours(6);
// the time of d is now set to 6:00:00 AM and i equals
// 1009260000000
```

4

setUTCMilliseconds()

The setUTCMilliseconds() method sets the number of milliseconds in the time of a Date object in universal time (UTC). UTC is basically the same as GMT. It takes one argument, an integer between 0 and 999. setMilliseconds() returns the adjusted date in millisecond format.

setMilliseconds() is available in JavaScript 1.2 and higher.

```
var d = new Date(2001,11,25);
// sets d to December 25th, 2001, 12:00:00:00 AM by default
var i = d.setUTCMilliseconds(500);
// the time of d is now set to 12:00:00:50 AM and i equals
// 1009256400500
```

setUTCMinutes()

The setUTCMinutes() method sets the minutes of the time in a Date object in universal time (UTC). UTC is basically the same as GMT. It takes one argument, which should be an integer between 1 and 31, and returns the new date in millisecond format.

setMinutes() is available in JavaScript 1.2 and later.

```
var d = new Date(2001,11,25);
// sets d to December 25th, 2001, 12:00:00:00 AM by default
var i = d.setUTCMinutes(30);
// the time of d is now set to 12:30:00:00 AM and i equals
// 1009258200000
```

setUTCMonth()

The setUTCMonth() method sets the month of a Date object in universal time (UTC). UTC is basically the same as GMT. It is passed one argument, which is an integer from 0, for January, to 11, for December.

setUTCMonth() is available in JavaScript 1.2 and later.

```
var d = new Date(2001,11,25);
// sets d to December 25th, 2001
var i = d. setUTCMonth(0);
// d is now set to January 25th, 2001 and i equals 980398800000
```

setUTCSeconds()

The setUTCSeconds() method sets the number of seconds in the time of a Date object in universal time (UTC). UTC is basically the same as GMT. It takes one argument, an integer that should be between 0 and 59.

`setUTCSeconds()` is available in JavaScript 1.2 and higher.

```
var d = new Date(2001,11,25);
// sets d to December 25th, 2001, 12:00:00:00 AM by default
var i = d.setUTCSeconds(30);
// the time of d is now set to 12:00:30:00 AM
// i equals 1009256430000 in JavaScript 1.2 and higher
```

setYear()

The `setYear()` method sets the year of a Date object. It takes one argument, the year in four-digit format or two-digit format for years after 1899 and before 2000.

In JavaScript 1.2 and higher, `setYear()` returns the new date in millisecond format. In JavaScript 1.0 and 1.1, `setYear()` returns nothing.

`setYear()` was introduced in JavaScript 1.0, and was deprecated in JavaScript 1.2 in favor of `setFullYear()`.

```
var d = new Date(2001,11,25);
// sets d to December 25th, 2001
var i = d.setYear(92);
// the year is now set to 1992
// i equals 725259600000 in JavaScript 1.2 and later
var i = d.setYear(2002);
// the year is now set to 2002
// i equals 1040792400000 in JavaScript 1.2 and later
```

toGMTString()

The `toGMTString()` method returns a string representation of a Date object converted to Greenwich Mean Time (GMT).

`toGMTString()` has one odd inconsistency. Netscape and early versions of Internet Explorer print "GMT" at the end of the date string, while Internet Explorer 4 prints "UTC" at the end of the string.

`toGMTString()` was introduced in JavaScript 1.0, and was deprecated in JavaScript 1.2 in favor of `toUTCString()`.

```
var d = new Date(2001,11,25);
// sets d to December 25th, 2001
var dString = d.toGMTString();
```

```
// dString equals
// "Tue, 25 Dec 2001 05:00:00 UTC" (IE 4)
// "Tue, 25 Dec 2001 05:00:00 GMT" (Netscape)
```

toLocaleString()

The `toLocaleString()` method returns a string representation of
a Date object using the local time zone, and date and time formatting
of the computer that executes the code. Because date and time
formatting differs widely across the world, this method can produce
very different results depending on where it's executed.

`toLocaleString()` is available in JavaScript 1.0 and higher.

```
var d = new Date(2001,11,25);
// sets d to December 25th, 2001
var dString = d.toLocaleString();
// dString equals "12/25/2001 00:00:00 in EST"
```

toString()

The `toString()` method returns a string representation of a Date
object using the local time zone of the computer that executes the
code. The formatting of the date is implementation dependent, but
doesn't necessarily use local date and time formatting. Because of
this, the results of this method can differ widely.

`toString()` is available in JavaScript 1.1 and higher.

```
var d = new Date(2001,11,25);
// sets d to December 25th, 2001
var dString = d.toString();
// dString equals
// "Tue Dec 25 00:00:00 EST 2001" (IE 4) or
// "Tue Dec 25 00:00:00 GMT-0500 (Eastern Standard Time) 2001"
     (Netscape)
```

toUTCString()

The `toUTCString()` method returns a string representation of a
Date object converted to universal time (UTC).

`toUTCString()` has one odd inconsistency. Netscape and early
versions of Internet Explorer print "GMT" at the end of the date
string, while Internet Explorer 4 prints "UTC" at the end of
the string.

`toUTCString()` is available in JavaScript 1.2 and higher.

```
var d = new Date(2001,11,25); // sets d to December 25th, 2001
var dString = d.toGMTString();
```

```
// dString equals "Tue, 25 Dec 2001 05:00:00 UTC" (IE 4) or
// "Tue, 25 Dec 2001 05:00:00 GMT" (Netscape)
```

valueOf()

The valueOf() method returns a millisecond representation of a Date object. This is the number of milliseconds between the date of a Date object and midnight, January 1, 1970 GMT. valueOf() behaves identically to getTime().

A millisecond representation of a date can be used to create a new Date object.

valueOf() is available in JavaScript 1.1 and higher.

```
var d = new Date(2001,11,25);
// sets d to December 25th, 2001
var i = Date.valueOf(d);
// i equals 1009256400000
var d2 = new Date(i);
// d2 is set to December 25th, 2001
```

UTC()

The Date.UTC() method converts date parameters to a date in millisecond format. These parameters are the same as the parameters passed to the Date constructor. Arguments are passed in this order: *year, month, day, hours, minutes, seconds, milliseconds.*

The *hours, minutes, seconds*, and *milliseconds* arguments are optional. *Milliseconds* are ignored in JavaScript 1.0 and 1.1.

Date.UTC() is available in JavaScript 1.0 and higher.

```
var i = Date.UTC(2001,11,25,0,0,0,0); // i equals 1009256400000
var d = new Date(i); // d2 is set to December 25th, 2001,
        0:00:00:00 UTC
```

eval()

The eval() method takes one argument, which is a string of JavaScript code to be executed. eval() executes the string of JavaScript code that is passed to it, and returns whatever value is returned by the last statement, if any value is returned.

When executed in Netscape 2.0 on Windows 3.1 platforms, eval() crashes Netscape.

`eval()` is available in JavaScript 1.0 and later and was included in the ECMA-262 specification.

```
var s = "var i = 32; i *= 2; alert(i);";
// creates the string, s, which contains JavaScript code
// eval(s);
// executes the code, s
// creates the value i, which equals 32, doubles it, then alerts i
```

Math

The Math object contains references to mathematical constants and functions. It's a static object, which means you can't create instances of the Math object with the `new` constructor, and all of the Math object's methods and properties are read-only.

The Math object is available in JavaScript 1.0 and higher, and was included in the ECMA-262 specification.

Table 4-5 summarizes the methods in the Math object, and Table 4-6 summarizes the properties. The following sections describe each method and property in more detail.

Method	Description	JavaScript Version	Notes
abs()	Calculates an absolute value	1.0, ECMA-262	Static method
acos()	Calculates an arc cosine	1.0, ECMA-262	Static method
asin()	Calculates an arc sine	1.0, ECMA-262	Static method
atan()	Calculates an arc tangent	1.0, ECMA-262	Static method

Table 4-5. Methods Available in the Math Object

4

Method	Description	JavaScript Version	Notes
atan2()	Calculates the angle from the X axis to a point	1.0, ECMA-262	Static method
ceil()	Rounds a number up	1.0, ECMA-262	Static method
cos()	Calculates a cosine	1.0, ECMA-262	Static method
exp()	Calculates an exponent of e	1.0, ECMA-262	Static method
floor()	Rounds a number down	1.0, ECMA-262	Static method
log()	Calculates a natural logarithm	1.0, ECMA-262	Static method
max()	Compares two numbers, returns the larger one	1.0, ECMA-262	Static method
min()	Compares two numbers, returns the smaller one	1.0, ECMA-262	Static method
pow()	Calculates a number raised to a given power	1.0, ECMA-262	Static method
random()	Returns a random number	1.0, ECMA-262	Static method
round()	Rounds a number to the nearest integer	1.0, ECMA-262	Static method
sin()	Calculates a sine	1.0, ECMA-262	Static method
sqrt()	Calculates a square root	1.0, ECMA-262	Static method
tan()	Calculates a tangent	1.0, ECMA-262	Static method

Table 4-5.   Methods Available in the Math Object *(continued)*

Property	Description	JavaScript Version	Notes
E	e, the base of the natural logarithm	1.0, ECMA-262	Read-only, static
LN10	The natural logarithm of 10	1.0, ECMA-262	Read-only, static
LN2	The natural logarithm of 2	1.0, ECMA-262	Read-only, static
LOG2E	The Base-2 (binary) logarithm of e	1.0, ECMA-262	Read-only, static
LOG10E	The natural logarithm of e	1.0, ECMA-262	Read-only, static
PI	π	1.0, ECMA-262	Read-only, static
SQRT1_2	1 divided by the square root of 2	1.0, ECMA-262	Read-only, static
SQRT2	The square root of 2	1.0, ECMA-262	Read-only, static

Table 4-6.   Properties Available in the Math Object

Math Methods and Properties

abs()

The abs() method returns the absolute value of a number. It takes one argument, which can be any numeric value.

abs() is available in JavaScript 1.0 and later and was included in the ECMA-262 specification.

```
var i = Math.abs(-33.337);
// i equals 33.337
```

Note that abs() is a static method that can only be called by executing Math.abs().

acos()

The acos() method returns the arccosine of a number. It takes one argument, which can be any numeric value between –1 and 1. The value that asin() returns is always between zero and π in radians, or NaN if the argument passed to acos() is out of range.

You can convert radians to degrees by dividing by
`((Math.PI*2)/360)`.

`acos()` is available in JavaScript 1.0 and higher, and was included
in the ECMA-262 specification.

```
var r = Math.acos(-1);
// get the arccosine of -1
var a = var a = r / ((Math.PI*2)/360);
// convert radians to degrees
```

Note that `acos()` is a static method that can only be called by
executing `Math.acos()`.

4

asin()

The `asin()` method calculates the arcsine of a number. It takes
one argument, which can be any numeric value between –1 and 1.
The value that `asin()` returns is always between $-\pi/2$ and $\pi/2$ in
radians, or `NaN` if the argument passed to `asin()` is out of range.

You can convert radians to degrees by dividing by
`((Math.PI*2)/360)`.

`asin()` is available in JavaScript 1.0 and higher, and was included
in the ECMA-262 specification.

```
var r = Math.asin(0.5); // calculate the arcsine of 35
var a = r / ((Math.PI*2)/360); // convert radians to degrees
```

Note that `atan()` is a static method that can only be called by
executing `Math.atan()`.

atan()

The `atan()` method calculates the arctangent of a number. It takes
one argument, which can be any numeric value, and returns the
arctangent of that number in radians.

You can convert radians to degrees by dividing by
`((Math.PI*2)/360)`.

`atan()` is available in JavaScript 1.0 and higher and was included
in the ECMA-262 specification.

```
var r = Math.atan(35); // calculate the arctangent of 35
var t = r / ((Math.PI*2)/360); // convert radians to degrees
```

Note that `atan()` is a static method that can only be called by
executing `Math.atan()`.

atan2()

The `atan2()` method calculates the distance between a point and the *X* axis. It takes two arguments, which are the x and y coordinates of a point. It returns an angle in radians that is the counterclockwise measurement from the positive *X* axis to the point.

You can convert radians to degrees by dividing by `((Math.PI*2)/360)`.

`atan2()` is available in JavaScript 1.0 and higher and was included in the ECMA-262 specification.

```
var r = Math.atan2(3,4);
// calculate the angle in radians
var a = r / ((Math.PI*2)/360);
// convert radians to degrees
```

Note that `atan2()` is a static method that can only be called by executing `Math.atan2()`.

ceil()

The `ceil()` method rounds a number up to the next whole number. It takes one argument, which can be any numeric value.

`ceil()` is available in JavaScript 1.0 and higher, and was included in the ECMA-262 specification.

```
var i = Math.ceil(23.253); // i equals 24
```

Note that `ceil()` is a static method that can only be called by executing `Math.ceil()`.

cos()

The `cos()` method calculates the cosine of an angle. It takes one argument, an angle in radians, and returns a value between –1 and 1.

You can convert degrees to radians by multiplying by `((Math.PI*2)/360)`.

`cos()` is available in JavaScript 1.0 and higher, and was included in the ECMA-262 specification.

```
var d = 35 * ((Math.PI*2)/360); // convert 35 degrees to radians
var c = Math.cos(d); // calculate the cosine of d
```

Note that `cos()` is a static method that can only be called by executing `Math.cos()`.

E

E is a read-only constant that represents the base of the natural logarithm. This value is approximately equal to 2.6183.

E is available in JavaScript 1.0 and higher, and was included in the ECMA-262 specification.

```
document.write(Math.E);
// writes "2.718281828459045"
```

Note that E is a constant, a read-only property that can only be referred to as Math.E.

4

exp()

The exp() method multiplies a number by *e*, the base of the natural logarithm. It takes one argument, which can be any numeric value.

exp() is available in JavaScript 1.0 and higher, and was included in the ECMA-262 specification.

```
var i = Math.exp(2);
// i equals 7.38905609893065
```

Note that exp() is a static method that can only be executed by calling Math.exp().

floor()

The floor() method rounds a number down to the previous whole number. It takes one argument, which can be any numeric value.

floor() is available in JavaScript 1.0 and later, and was included in the ECMA-262 specification.

```
var i = Math.floor(23.253); // i equals 23
```

Note that floor() is a static method that can only be called by executing Math.floor().

LN2

The LN2 property stores the value of the natural logarithm of 2, or $\log_e 2$. The value of LN2 is approximately 0.69314.

LN2 is available in JavaScript 1.0 and higher, and was included in the ECMA-262 specification.

```
document.write(Math.LN2); // writes "0.6931471805599453"
```

Note that LN2 is a constant, a read-only property that can only be referred to as Math.LN2.

LN10

The LN10 property stores the value of the natural logarithm of 10, or $\log_e 10$. The value of LN10 is approximately 2.30258.

LN10 is available in JavaScript 1.0 and higher, and was included in the ECMA-262 specification.

```
document.write(Math.LN10);
// writes "2.302585092994046"
```

Note that LN10 is a constant, a read-only property that can only be referred to as Math.LN10.

log()

The log() method calculates the natural logarithm of a number, or $\log_e x$. It takes one argument, which can be any number greater than zero.

To generate a number greater than zero, you can use the Math.abs() method.

log() is available in JavaScript 1.0 and higher, and was included in the ECMA-262 specification.

```
var i = log(2);
// calculates the natural log of 2
var i = log(2) * Math.LOG2E; // calculate the base-2 logarithm of 2
var i = log(2) * Math.LOG10E; // calculate the base-10 logarithm
        of 2
```

Note that log() is a static method that can only be called by executing Math.log().

LOG10E

The LOG10E stores the Base-10 value of e, or $\log_{10} e$. The value of LOG10E is approximately 0.43429.

LOG10E is available in JavaScript 1.0 and higher, and was included in the ECMA-262 specification.

```
document.write(Math.LOG10E); // writes "0.4342944819032518"
```

Note that LOG10E is a constant, a read-only property that can only be referred to as Math.LOG10E.

LOG2E

The LOG2E stores the binary, or Base-2, value of e, or $\log_2 e$. The value of LOG2E is approximately 1.44269.

LOG2E is available in JavaScript 1.0 and higher, and was included in the ECMA-262 specification.

```
document.write(Math.LOG2E);
// writes "1.4426950408889633"
```

Note that LOG2E is a constant, a read-only property that can only be referred to as Math.LOG2E.

max ( )

The max() method calculates the larger of two values. It takes two arguments, any two numeric values, and returns the larger one.

max() is available in JavaScript 1.0 and higher, and was included in the ECMA-262 specification.

```
var i = Math.max(56,65);
// i equals 65
```

Note that max() is a static method that can only be called by executing Math.max().

min ( )

The min() method calculates the smaller of two values. It takes two arguments, any two numeric values, and returns the smaller one.

min() is available in JavaScript 1.0 and higher, and was included in the ECMA-262 specification.

```
var i = Math.min(56,65);
// i equals 56
```

Note that min() is a static method that can only be called by executing Math.min().

PI

The PI property stores the value *pi*, which is the ratio of the circumference of any circle to its diameter. The value of PI is approximately 3.14159.

PI is available in JavaScript 1.0 and higher, and was included in the ECMA-262 specification.

```
document.write(Math.PI);
// writes "3.141592653589793"
```

Note that PI is a constant, a read-only property that can only be referred to as Math.PI.

pow()

The pow() method raises a number to a given power. It takes two arguments. The first argument is the number that is to be raised to a power, and the second argument is the power by which the first number will be raised.

pow() is available in JavaScript 1.0 and higher, and was included in the ECMA-262 specification.

```
var i = Math.pow(2,4); // i equals 16
```

pow() can also be used to calculate the root of a number.

```
var i = Math.pow(2,1/3); // i equals the cube root of 2
```

Note that pow() is a static method that can only be called by executing Math.pow().

random()

The random() method generates and returns a pseudorandom number between zero and one. It takes no arguments.

random() is available in JavaScript 1.0 and higher, and was included in the ECMA-262 specification.

```
var i = Math.random();
// i equals a pseudorandom number between 0 and 1
var i = Math.random()*7
// i equals a pseudorandom number between 0 and 7
```

Note that random() is a static method that can only be called by executing Math.random().

round()

The round() method rounds a number to the nearest whole number. It takes one argument, which can be any numeric value. Half numbers are rounded up; for example, 1.5 is rounded to 2.

round() is available in JavaScript 1.0 and higher, and was included in the ECMA-262 specification.

```
var i = Math.round(23.253); // i equals 23
```

Note that round() is a static method that can only be called by executing Math.round().

To round numbers up and down specifically, use the `Math.ceil()` and `Math.floor()` methods.

sin()

The `sin()` method calculates the cosine of an angle. It takes one argument, an angle in radians, and returns a value between –1 and 1.

You can convert degrees to radians by multiplying by `((Math.PI*2)/360)`.

`sin()` is available in JavaScript 1.0 and higher, and was included in the ECMA-262 specification.

```
var d = 35 * ((Math.PI*2)/360); // convert 35 degrees to radians
var c = Math.sin(d); // calculate the sine of d
```

Note that `sin()` is a static method that can only be called by executing `Math.sin()`.

sqrt()

The `sqrt()` method calculates the square root of a number. It takes one argument, which can be any numeric value.

`sqrt()` is available in JavaScript 1.0 and higher, and was included in the ECMA-262 specification.

```
var i = Math.sqrt(9); // i equals 3
```

Note that `sqrt()` is a static method that can only be called by executing `Math.sqrt()`.

The `Math.pow()` method can be used to calculate roots other than the square root.

SQRT1_2

The `SQRT1_2` property stores the value of the square root of one divided by two. This is the reciprocal of the square root of two. The value of `SQRT1_2` is approximately 0.70710.

`SQRT1_2` is available in JavaScript 1.0 and higher, and was included in the ECMA-262 specification.

```
document.write(Math.SQRT1_2); // writes "0.7071067811865476"
```

Note that SQRT1_2 is a constant, a read-only property that can only be referred to as Math.SQRT1_2.

SQRT2

The SQRT2 property stores the value of the square root of two. The value of SQRT2 is approximately 1.41421.

SQRT2 is available in JavaScript 1.0 and higher, and was included in the ECMA-262 specification.

```
document.write(Math.SQRT2); // writes " 1.4142135623730951"
```

Note that SQRT2 is a constant, a read-only property that can only be referred to as Math.SQRT2.

tan()

The tan() method calculates the tangent of an angle. It takes one argument, which is an angle measured in radians.

You can convert degrees to radians by multiplying by ((Math.PI*2)/360).

tan() is available in JavaScript 1.0 and higher, and was included in the ECMA-262 specification

```
var d = 35 * ((Math.PI*2)/360);
// convert 35 degrees to radians
var t = Math.tan(d);
// calculate the tangent of d
```

Note that tan() is a static method that can only be called by executing Math.tan().

MimeType

The MimeType object is a good way to find out what types of applications are supported by the user's browser—either by programs on the PC or via plug-ins. MIME Type refers to a format of data. Unfortunately, the MimeType object is only supported by Netscape 3 and above.

Table 4-7 summarizes the properties in the MimeType object.

The MimeType object uses an array, navigator.mimeTypes[], that is indexed numerically or with the name of the desired MIME type. The following script will allow you to view all of your MIME types:

```
var num = 0;
document.write("<pre>");
while ("navigator.mimeTypes[num]" != "undefined")
  {
  MyMIME = navigator.mimeTypes[num];
  document.write("Index:\t\t" + num + "\n");
  document.write("mimeTypes:\t" + MyMIME + "\n");
  document.write("description:\t" + MyMIME.description + "\n");
  document.write("enabledPlugin:\t" + MyMIME.enabledPlugin + "\n");
  document.write("suffixes:\t" + MyMIME.suffixes + "\n");
  document.write("type:\t\t" + MyMIME.type + "\n\n\n");
  num++;
  }
document.write("</pre>");
```

Property	Description	JavaScript Version	Notes
description	Description of the MIME type	Client-side Navigator 3	Read-only
enabledPlugin	Plug-in that handles the MIME type	Client-side Navigator 3	Read-only
suffixes	Common file suffixes for a MIME type	Client-side Navigator 3	Read-only
type	Name of a MIME type	Client-side Navigator 3	Read-only

Table 4-7. Properties Available in the MimeType Object

MimeType Properties

description

The description property is an easy-to-read description of the data type described in the MIME type.

```
document.write(navigator.mimeTypes
  ["application/pdf"].description);
// this returns: Acrobat
```

enabledPlugin

The enabledPlugin property determines whether there is a plug-in available to handle the requested MIME type. It returns [object Plugin] if a plug-in is available, or null if not.

```
document.write(navigator.mimeTypes
  ["application/pdf"].enabledPlugin);
// this returns: [object Plugin]
// only if I have the Acrobat Plug-in available.
```

suffixes

The suffixes property returns a list of extensions supported by the MIME type it is passed. The file extensions are comma delimited.

```
document.write(navigator.mimeTypes["text/html"].
  suffixes);
// on my computer, this returns: html, htm, shtml
```

type

The type property returns a unique string that distinguishes between two MIME types. The type property may be used as an index to access elements of the navigator.mimeType[] array.

```
document.write(navigator.mimeTypes[31].suffixes);
// on my computer, this is listed as: text/xml
```

Number

The Number object provides support for numbers. It's usually not necessary to explicitly create Number objects, but it's supported nonetheless. The Number object also contains JavaScript-specific constant numbers, such as the minimum and maximum value of any number, and negative and positive infinity. These constants are static and read-only. Table 4-8 summarizes the constants in the Number object.

Number contains only one method, toString(), which returns the value of a Number object as a string in a specified base (radix).

The Number object is available in JavaScript 1.1 and later, and was included in the ECMA-262 specification.

The Number Constructor

A Number object can be created with a new statement. The constructor takes one argument, a numeric value.

The Number constructor is available in JavaScript 1.1 and higher, and was included in the ECMA-262 specification.

```
var n = new Number(112); // n is now set to 112
```

Number Methods and Properties

Following are descriptions of the methods and properties available in the Number object to date.

MAX_VALUE

MAX_VALUE is a read-only constant that equals the largest number that JavaScript can represent. This is approximately 1.79E+308. The only number larger than MAX_VALUE is POSITIVE_INFINITY.

Constant	Description
MAX_VALUE	The largest number that can be represented
MIN_VALUE	The smallest number that can be represented
NaN	A special non-number number
NEGATIVE_INFINITY	Infinite value, returned when a number exceeds MIN_VALUE
POSITIVE_INFINITY	Infinite value, returned when a number exceeds MAX_VALUE

Table 4-8. Constants Available in the Number Object

MAX_VALUE is available in JavaScript 1.1 and higher, and was included in the ECMA-262 specification.

```
var bigNum = Number.MAX_VALUE;
```

Note that MAX_VALUE is a static variable; so if you created a Number object called n, you wouldn't be able to access n.MAX_VALUE. The MAX_VALUE constant can only be referred to as Number.MAX_VALUE.

MIN_VALUE

MIN_VALUE is a read-only constant that equals the smallest non-zero number that JavaScript can represent. This is approximately 5e-324. The only number smaller than MIN_VALUE is NEGATIVE_INFINITY.

MIN_VALUE is available in JavaScript 1.1 and higher, and was included in the ECMA-262 specification.

```
var smallNum = Number.MIN_VALUE;
```

Note that MIN_VALUE is a static variable; so if you created a Number object called n, you wouldn't be able to access n.MIN_VALUE. The MIN_VALUE constant can only be referred to as Number.MIN_VALUE.

NaN

NaN is a read-only constant. It stands for Not-a-Number. It is returned by a method such as parseInt() and parseFloat() when a mathematical calculation can't be returned.

NaN is available in JavaScript 1.1 and higher, and was included in the ECMA-262 specification.

NaN can't be used practically in a test, because it isn't equal to any number or itself. To test for NaN, see the method, isNaN().

```
var i = 51;
var test = (i == Number.NaN); // test equals false
```

Note that NaN is a static variable; so if you created a Number object called n, you wouldn't be able to access n.NaN. The NaN constant can be referred to as either NaN or Number.NaN.

NEGATIVE_INFINITY

NEGATIVE_INFINITY is a read-only constant that represents negative infinity. If this number is returned by a method, it usually means there has been an overflow error.

NEGATIVE_INFINITY is available in JavaScript 1.1 and higher, and was included in the ECMA-262 specification.

```
var negativeInfinity = Number.NEGATIVE_INFINITY
```

Note that NEGATIVE_INFINITY is a static variable; so if you created a Number object called n, you wouldn't be able to access n.NEGATIVE_INFINITY. The NEGATIVE_INFINITY constant can only be referred to as Number.NEGATIVE_INFINITY.

POSITIVE_INFINITY

POSITIVE_INFINITY is a read-only constant that represents infinity. If this number is returned by a method, it usually means there has been an overflow error.

POSITIVE_INFINITY is available in JavaScript 1.1 and higher, and was included in the ECMA-262 specification.

```
var infinity = Number.POSITIVE_INFINITY
```

Note that POSITIVE_INFINITY is a static variable; so if you created a Number object called n, you wouldn't be able to access n.POSITIVE_INFINITY. The POSITIVE_INFINITY constant can only be referred to as Number.POSITIVE_INFINITY.

toString()

The toString() method of a Number object returns a string representation of the value of a Number object. toString() takes one argument, which can be a base, or radix, between 2 and 36. If no argument is passed to toString(), it uses Base-10, which is the base that most people use anyway.

toString() is available in JavaScript 1.1 and higher, and was included in the ECMA-262 specification.

```
var i = 32;
var s = i.toString(); // s equals "32"
var s = i.toString(2); // s equals "100000" (binary)
var s = i.toString(8); // s equals "40" (base 8)
```

toString() can also be used to print the Number object 's constants in a more readable format.

```
var s = Number.MAX_VALUE.toString();
// s equals "1.7976931348623157e+308"
var s = Number.MIN_VALUE.toString(); // s equals "5e-324"
var s = Number.NaN; // s equals "NaN"
var s = Number.NEGATIVE_INFINITY; // s equals "-Infinity"
var s = Number.POSITIVE_INFINITY; // s equals "Infinity"
```

parseFloat()

The `parseFloat()` method converts a string into a floating-point number. It takes one argument, a string, and returns either the first number in the string or `NaN` if no number is found.

`parseFloat()` is available in JavaScript 1.0 and was included in the ECMA-262 specification. In JavaScript 1.0, `NaN` wasn't supported, so `parseFloat()` returned zero when it encountered a non-number string.

```
var s = "3.14 radians";
var i = parseFloat(s);
// i equals 3.14
s = "pi radians (3.14)";
var i = parseFloat(s);
// i equals NaN in JavaScript 1.1, 0 in v1.0
```

parseInt()

The `parseInt()` method converts a string into a floating-point number. It takes two arguments. The first is a string that begins with a number to convert to an integer. The second is an optional base, or radix, for the return value. If this is left blank, the answer is Base-10, the way most people like it. The value that is returned is an integer.

If no number is found at the beginning of the string, `parseInt()` returns `NaN`.

`parseInt()` is available in JavaScript 1.0 and was included in the ECMA-262 specification. In JavaScript 1.0, `NaN` wasn't supported, so `parseInt()` returned zero when it encountered a non-number string.

```
var s = "3.14 radians";
var i = parseInt(s);
// i equals 3
s = "pi radians (3.14)";
var i = parseInt(s);
// i equals NaN in JavaScript 1.1, 0 in JavaScript 1.0
```

RegExp

The `RegExp` object supports regular expressions, which are used to match patterns of text and assist in search-and-replace operations. There are several different implementations of regular expressions; JavaScript uses the same syntax as the programming language Perl.

`RegExp` is supported in JavaScript 1.2 and later, and was included in the ECMA-262 specification.

4

`RegExp` objects may be created using the `RegExp()` constructor. The literal syntax of `RegExp` may be encoded into JavaScript programs. Patterns are held between two slashes, and the second slash (/) may be followed by a letter, to change the functionality of the pattern. Here are three examples of several regular expressions:

```
/<a.href=/i     /[a-z][A-Z]/g      /<br>\n/
```

Defining Regular Expressions

Regular expressions may be created literally or with the `RegExp()` constructor. Both of these techniques only work in JavaScript 1.2 and higher, because regular expressions aren't available in previous versions.

The RegExp Constructor

The variable `MyExpression` is assigned a new RegExp object here. The pattern that it will match must start with `<a href`. You may also define a variable using the `RegExp()` constructor.

```
var MyExpression = new RegExp("^<a href");
```

Regular Expression Literals

Any string literal regular expression may be set to a variable. The difference is that regular expressions are enclosed in slashes (/) rather than single or double quotes.

```
var MyExpression = /^<a href/a
```

Pattern Matching

Pattern matching describes the basic function of regular expressions. Pattern matching allows RegExp to distinguish strings of letters, numbers, spaces, and symbols, from other text. Simple pattern matching is quite easy, while looking for specific things may be quite a task. If you have not used pattern matching before you may be confused at first, but after awhile, you will gain an extremely powerful tool.

Literal Characters

Literal characters fall into several groups: characters, metacharacters, special characters, special numbers, and character classes. Each serves a certain function, discussed here.

Characters   Alphabetic and numeric characters match themselves literally. This is also true for most other characters, with several exceptions that fall into a group called metacharacters, explained next.

Table 4-9 shows three examples of character matching.

Metacharacters   Characters that serve special functions are called *metacharacters*. In order to match these characters, shown in Table 4-10, you must type a backslash " \ " before the character.

Special Characters   Characters that are not letters, numbers, or symbols are categorized as special characters. They are shown in Table 4-11.

Example Regular Expression	Matches	Doesn't Match
/bob/	bob, bobby, !bob, bob123	b, bo, bo1
/123/	11233, 12333, 11123	4, 15, 1223
/!@#/	!@#, !!@#, !@##	*, !@@#

Table 4-9.   Matching Characters with Regular Expressions

Character Name	Metacharacter	Match
Open curly bracket	\ {	{
Closed curly bracket	\ }	}
Open square bracket	\ [	[
Closed square bracket	\ ]	]
Open parenthesis	\ (	(
Closed parenthesis	\ )	)
Caret	\ ^	^
Dollar sign	\ $	$
Period	\ .	.
Pipe	\			
Asterisk (star)	\ *	*
Plus	\ +	+
Question mark	\ ?	?
Slash	\ /	/
Backslash	\ \	\

Table 4-10.   Regular Expression Metacharacters

Special Numbers   Literal numbers may also be octal or hexadecimal numbers, as well as control characters. Table 4-12 gives some examples.

Character	Match
\ f	Form feed
\ n	Carriage return
\ t	Tab
\ v	Vertical tab

Table 4-11.   Regular Expression Special Characters

Expression	Number Type
\###	Octal numbers
\x##	Hexadecimal numbers
\u####	Unicode numbers
\cX	Control characters

Table 4-12. Regular Expression Special Numbers

Octal numbers are a Base-8 number system, which is a single-digit system that includes the numbers 0, 1, 2, 3, 4, 5, 6, and 7. The number 10 follows 7, and 20 follows 17.

Hexadecimal numbers are a Base-16 number system, which includes the numbers 0, 1, 2, 3, 4, 5, 6, 7, 8, 9, A, B, C, D, E, and F. The letters A–F represent the numbers 10–15. Hexadecimal numbers are represented in JavaScript as double digits: 01, 0A, AA, FC.

The Unicode numbering system is made up of four hexadecimal numbers. It is currently used to display non-English characters.

Control characters (shown in Table 4-13) are special nonprinting characters, originally used to control teletype machines. Now they are used to control display monitors, printers, and other devices.

Character Classes Groups of character literals are called *character classes*, which are commonly used to match a series of character literals. Character classes are useful in matching words or groups of characters. Table 4-14 lists the available character classes; Table 4-15 gives some examples of how they are used.

Expression	Matches
/\120/	The letter P
/x23	The # symbol
\u05E5	? (Hebrew letter Final Tsadi)
\cI	A tab

Table 4-13. Regular Expression Control Characters

Character Class	Matches
[...]	Any single character within the brackets
[^...]	Any single character except the characters in the brackets
.	Any character except the carriage return "\n" character
\w	Any word
\W	Any non-word
\s	Any whitespace
\S	Any non-whitespace
\d	Any number
\D	Any non-number
[\b]	A backspace (rare)

Table 4-14. Regular Expression Character Classes

Example	Matches	Doesn't Match
/fact[oid]/	factoids, factitious	fact, facts, factless
/bob[^s]/	bobby, bobcat	bob, bobs
/b.t/	bit, bitrate, but, butter, b@test.com	bi, b, b\nt
/\w/	<a href, food, word	., \s, !, @,], \t
/\W/	!@!#!, \n, \t	foot, big feet, size=large
/\s/	best in town, fast cars, <a href	small, medium, large
/\S/	small, medium, large	best in town, fast cars, <a href
/\d/	123, 321, 1245512, abc123	color=green, word, letters
/\D/	color=green, word, letters	123, 321, 1245512, abc123

Table 4-15. Examples of Regular Expression Character Classes

Repeating Characters   The preceding examples may lead
you to believe that matching many characters would require
very large regular expressions. Thankfully, there is an easier
way. Repeating characters are commonly used to match
strings of repeating characters, as shown in Table 4-16.

As you can see, repeating characters will make your regular
expression much easier to manage. Table 4-17 gives several
examples.

Grouping and OR   Grouping allows you to split up regular
expressions. This is useful when matching more complex patterns.
To group a regular expression, all you need to do is enclose it in
parenthesis. For example,

```
var MyGroup = /<a\s href="(.+)">(\w+)</a>/a
```

The `MyGroup` expression contains two groups. The first group
checks for one or more characters, while the second checks for
one or more words.

Grouping is commonly used with OR, which allows you to match
different groups of possibilities. For example,

```
var OrGroup = /((bgcolor="(.+)")|(background="(.+\.(gif|jpg))"))/
```

Character	Matches
X{Y,Z}	X at least Y times, but not more than Z
X{Y,}	X Y or more times
X{Y}	X Y times
X?	Zero or one occurrence of X; same as X{0,1}
X+	One or more occurrences of X; same as X{1,}
X*	Zero or more occurrences of X; same as X{0,}

Table 4-16.   Repeating Characters with Regular Expressions

Example	Matches
`/\s.{2,5}\./`	Whitespace followed by two to five characters ending with a period
`/\w{3,}/`	Three or more words
`/a{4}/`	aaaa, aaaaxyz, aaaa1234 (remember the `/bob/` example)
`/ar{5}gh!/`	arrrrrgh!
`/\w?\./`	Zero or more words followed by a period
`/\(\d+\)/`	(1), (123), (32495), (234658)
`/[a-z][A-Z]*/`	Any string containing any letter or no letters; will not match `"11"`

Table 4-17.   Examples of Repeating Characters with Regular Expressions

The preceding expression will match any of the following strings:

```
bgcolor="blue"              bgcolor="black"
background="waves.jpg"      background="image.gif"
background="fruit.gif"      background="cloud.jpg"
```

The `OrGroup` variable in the preceding matches either `bgcolor` or `background`, which may be a `gif` or a `jpg`.

Parts of groups may be referred to by a `\#`. The `OrGroup` variable in the previous code has a total of six subexpressions, which in turn are labeled as `\1` through `\6`. They are counted starting with one at the first open parenthesis and moving right, as follows:

```
$1   (bgcolor="(.+)")|(background="(.+\.(gif|jpg))")
$2   bgcolor="(.+)"
$3   .+
$4   background="(.+\.(gif|jpg))"
$5   .+\.(gif|jpg)
$6   gif|jpg
```

When using subexpressions, remember that they refer to the text matched, not the actual expression.

```
var SubRegExp = /(a|b|c) is the letter $1/;
// matches: a is the letter a
// does not match: a is the letter b
```

Current implementations of JavaScript are still very buggy with subexpressions, and you may want to avoid them. For example, note the following variable, which is much like the preceding one:

```
var BrokenSub = /(a|b|c)\s\w+\s$1/;
// This should match: a is the letter a
// It actually doesn't match anything.
```

Let's break down this example and look at what we are trying to match:

Expression	Matches
(a│b│c)	Any one of these letters
\s	One space
\w+	One or more words
\s	One space
$1	The matched letter

This Regular Expression also uses several special characters:

Character	Matches
│	One expression or the other, may be used in conjunction with subexpressions
(. . .)	A group of expressions
$#	Refers to a subexpression; matches the characters matched by that subexpression

Position Matching   All the preceding examples deal with matching a string of text. Position matching deals with matching the exact place in text: starts with, ends with, and so on. Position matching is very useful in matching bare words, as we saw earlier where /bob/ matched "bobby" and "bobbi," and if you only wanted to match "bob," you could use /^bob$/.

The caret symbol "^" demands that the match starts with the expression that follows it, while the dollar sign "$" demands that the match ends with the expression that it follows.

```
var Match1 = /</a>$/a;
var Match2 = /^<a href=/a;
```

The variable `Match1` matches a string that ends with `</a>`, while the `Match2` variable only matches a string that begins with `<a href=`.

Further, position matching includes matching invisible space. An invisible space is usually the space between two characters, but also may be the space before a character on a newline or the space after a character at the end of a line. To use these invisible characters, regular expressions incorporate the \b and \B characters. Here are some examples:

Expression	Matches
/a\b./	a c, a@domain.com, a word
/\w+\b\./	Invisible characters are easy to learn.
/\bWord\b/	Word
/\b\d\B/	2355asdf
/(\B)555\1/	abc555abc

Global Search, Case Insensitivity, and Multiline Input

Regular expressions support two attributes: i and g. You may use either attribute or both by appending them to the end of your expression: /bob/ig. The i attribute specifies that the text that you are matching be case insensitive. The g attribute will match your pattern globally, wherein it matches every occurrence of your pattern in a string of text.

The regular expression constructor handles these attributes in the same way, but the code looks a little different. For example,

```
var Expression1 = /^<a.href/ig;
// is the same as
var Expression2 = ("^<a.href", "gi");
```

Both of these expressions match a line starting with <a href, <A HREF, <A Href, and so forth.

Matching multiline input requires setting the multiline property of the RegExp() constructor. The multiline property will match strings, even if they have a newline in them. To enable the multiline property, simply set it to true.

```
RegExp.multiline = true;
```

Here is an example of matching multiline values with regular expressions:

Expression	Matches
/<\/a>^/	<a href="index.html>link</a>\nmore text

When using the multiline property in conjunction with a TextArea object, JavaScript automatically sets the property to true, but resets it to false when the event handler exits. It is a good idea always to set it to true if you plan to use it at all.

Matching Memory

Regular Expressions may also match and may be recalled later. These matches are recalled from the resulting array's elements, [1], ..., [n]. These Regular Expressions will be discussed further in later sections. See Table 4-18 for basic examples.

RegExp Methods

String Methods

There are several string methods for regular expressions: search(), replace(), match(), and split(). Each increases the functionality of JavaScript regular expressions.

search()   The search() method allows you to find the character position of the text you are trying to match. For instance,

```
var TextString = "I drive a small car.";
var SearchString = /c+/;
document.write(TextString.search(SearchString));
```

This returns the number 16, because the letter c is the 16th character. Remember that when you count, you always start with 0. If nothing was matched, the string() method returns -1.

Example	Type	Match
(bob)	Capturing parenthesis	Matches bob and remembers the match
(?:bob)	Noncapturing parenthesis	Matches bob, but does not remember the match
bob(?=sam)		Matches bob if followed by sam
bob(?!sam)		Matches bob if not followed by sam

Table 4-18. Matching Memory with Regular Expressions

replace() The replace() method is used for searching and replacing. You can simply pass it a regular expression and the text you would like to replace it with.

```
var TextString = "I drive a small car."
var Replacement = TextString.replace(/small/, "large");
document.write(Replacement);
```

This returns the sentence: I drive a large car.

Using replace() in conjunction with subexpressions adds another level of usefulness. The following code is good for changing a formatted phone number into a string of numbers.

```
var phonenumber = "(505) 555-1234";
var regexp = /\(((\d{3})\)\s(\d{3})-(\d{4})/;
document.write(phonenumber.replace(regexp, "$1$2$3"));
```

As you can see, the subexpressions $1, $2, $3 are used to call each block of numbers. This script prints 5055551234.

match() The match() method is for, you guessed it, matching. It will return the first match that it is passed, unless the g attribute is set. Whether or not you use the g attribute, the data is stored in an array.

```
var phonenumber = "(505) 555-1234";
var regexp = /\d{3}/;
```

```
var match = phonenumber.match(regexp);
document.write(match);
// this returns 505
document.write(match[0]);
// this returns 505 as well
```

The match() method has three properties: length, index, and input. As it does in normal arrays, the length property returns the number of characters in a particular element. The index property returns the character position of the final match, if using the g attribute. Finally, the input property returns the text that was passed to match().

```
var phonenumber = "(505) 555-1234";
var regexp = /\d{3,}/g;
var match = phonenumber.match(regexp);

document.write(match[2].length);
// returns 4
document.write(match.index);
// returns 10
document.write(match.input);
// returns (505) 555-1234
```

split()   The split() method is used for splitting up a line of data into an array. I have found that people like to enter phone numbers in various ways, so here's a quick regular expression I use to regulate phone number information:

```
var phonenumber1 = "703-555-4321";
var phonenumber2 = "703.555.1234";
var phonenumber3 = "703 555 2231";
var phonenumber4 = "(703) 555.4112";
var regexp = /\(|\)*(\.|-|\s)/g;
document.write(phonenumber1.split(regexp));
// returns 703,555,4321
document.write(phonenumber2.split(regexp));
// returns 703,555,1234
document.write(phonenumber3.split(regexp));
// returns 703,555,2231
document.write(phonenumber4.split(regexp));
// returns 703,555,4112
```

Of course, you can also retrieve part of the array. In the preceding example, you could use `phonenumber4.split(regexp)[2]` and only return `4112`.

RegExp Object

As we learned in the "Defining Regular Expressions" section, the RegExp object allows you to create regular expressions. You may also include the g, i, and gi attributes. Also, you must use the escape character (\) when using a backslash. For example,

```
var Word = new RegExp("I use JavaScript\\.", "i");
// matches the given phrase, ignoring case.
// is the same as: /I use JavaScript\./i
```

RegExp Object Methods

compile()   The first method is `compile()`, which is used to change the contents of a RegExp object.

```
Word.compile("\\w", "gi");
// changes the Word RegExp object to match any word globally,
// ignoring case.
// is the same as: /\w/gi
```

test()   The `test()` method is similar to the string `match()` method, though it returns true or false, instead of the text matched.

```
var regexp = new RegExp("SMALL\\sCAR", "i");
document.write(regexp.test("I drive a small car."));
// this returns: true
```

exec()   The `exec()` method returns the text matched, plus it updates several properties and indexes, which provide detailed information.

```
MyExpression = new RegExp ("\\B(car)\\B", "g");
ThisArray = MyExpression.exec("I have many scars from car wrecks.");
```

Table 4-19 shows the properties and indexes that the `exec()` method changes, for the preceding example.

Object	Property or Index	Description	Example
ThisArray		The matched string and remembered substrings	car, car
	index	The index matching the input string	13
	input	The passed string	I have many scars from car wrecks.
	[0]	The last matched characters	car
MyExpression	lastIndex	The index in which to start the next match	16
	source	The expression matched	\B(car)\B
	global	A Boolean value that determines whether the g attribute is set	true
	ignoreCase	A Boolean value that determines whether the i attribute is set	false
RegExp	lastMatch	The last matched characters	car
	leftContext	The substring preceding the most recent match	I have many s
	rightContext	The substring following the most recent match	s from car wrecks.
	multiline	A Boolean value that determines whether the string should be treated as a single line or as multiple lines separated by newline characters	false

Table 4-19.   Properties and Indexes Changed by exec()

Internet Explorer will display undefined for the following properties: lastIndex, global, ignoreCase, lastMatch, leftContext, rightContext, and multiline. They are not currently supported by that browser.

Also, the `test()` method will return the same `lastIndex`, `source`, `global`, `ignoreCase`, `lastMatch`, `leftContext`, and `rightContext` properties as `exec()` does.

Finally, if your search fails, the `lastIndex` property will reset to 0. If you are performing multiple searches, it is important to reset the `lastIndex` property to 0, so that your next search will start at 0 rather than the current value.

```
MyExpression.lastIndex = 0;
```

4

String

The String object provides support for strings, which are simply a group of characters. Strings are a basic data type in JavaScript.

Many of the String objects and functions simply return the contents of a String object with HTML formatting. Others manipulate and search strings, and perform other useful tasks.

The String object is available in JavaScript 1.0 and later, and some features are new in JavaScript 1.1 and 1.2. The String object is included in the ECMA specification.

Table 4-20 summarizes the methods and properties in the String object.

Method/ Property	Description	JavaScript Version	Notes
`anchor()`	Formats a string as a named anchor	1.0	Generates non-XHTML-compliant code
`big()`	Formats a string with `<BIG>` tags	1.0	Generates non-XHTML-compliant code
`blink()`	Formats a string with `<BLINK>` tags	1.0	Generates non-XHTML-compliant code

Table 4-20.   Methods and Properties Available in the String Object

Method/ Property	Description	JavaScript Version	Notes
bold()	Formats a string with `<B>` tags	1.0	Generates non-XHTML-compliant code
charAt()	Returns the character at a given location in a string	1.0, ECMA-262	Uses ISO-Latin-1 in early versions of Netscape 4
charCodeAt()	Returns the character code of a character at a given location in a string	1.2, ECMA-262	Uses ISO-Latin-1 in early versions of Netscape 4
concat()	Concatenates one or more strings onto a String object	1.2, ECMA-262	
fixed()	Formats a string with `<TT>` tags	1.0	
fontcolor()	Formats a string as a given color with `<FONT>` tags	1.0	Generates non-XHTML-compliant code
fontsize()	Formats a string as a given size with `<FONT>` tags	1.0	Generates non-XHTML-compliant code
fromCharCode()	Creates a string from Unicode values	1.2, ECMA-262	Static method, uses ISO-Latin-1 in early versions of Netscape 4
indexOf()	Returns the starting index of a given substring	1.0, ECMA-262	
italics()	Formats a string with `<I>` tags	1.0	Generates non-XHTML-compliant code
lastIndexOf()	Returns the last index of a given substring	1.0, ECMA-262	
length	The length in characters of a string	1.0, ECMA-262	
link()	Formats a string as a hyperlink	1.0	Generates non-XHTML-compliant code
match()	Searches a string for one or more regular expression matches	1.2, ECMA-262	

Table 4-20. Methods and Properties Available in the String Object *(continued)*

Method/ Property	Description	JavaScript Version	Notes
replace()	Replaces any pattern matching a given regular expression with a substring	1.2, ECMA-262	
search()	Searches a string for a regular expression	1.2, ECMA-262	
slice()	Returns a substring of a string	1.2, ECMA-262	
small()	Formats a string with <SMALL> tags	1.0	Generates non-XHTML-compliant code
split()	Returns a substring at a given set of beginning and ending characters	1.1, ECMA-262	Only supports regular expressions in JavaScript 1.2 and later
strike()	Formats a string with <STRIKE> tags	1.0	Generates non-XHTML-compliant code
sub()	Formats a string with <SUB> tags	1.0	Generates non-XHTML-compliant code
substr()	Returns a substring at a given set of beginning and ending characters	1.2, ECMA-262	
substring()	Returns a substring at a given set of beginning and ending characters	1.0, ECMA-262	
sup()	Formats a string with <SUP> tags	1.0	Generates non-XHTML-compliant code
toLowerCase()	Formats a string as lowercase	1.0, ECMA-262	
toUpperCase()	Formats a string as uppercase	1.0, ECMA-262	

Table 4-20.   Methods and Properties Available in the String Object *(continued)*

Creating Strings

Instances of the String object can be created either explicitly or implicitly. In JavaScript 1.0, they can only be created implicitly.

The String Constructor

To create a new String object, you can use a `new` statement. The String constructor has one optional argument, which is the initial value of a string. If this argument is left out, an empty string is created.

The String constructor is available in JavaScript 1.1 and higher, and was included in the ECMA-262 specification.

```
var s = new String("The quick brown fox ...");
// creates a String object set to "The quick brown fox ..."
var s = new String();
// creates an empty String object
```

Creating Strings in JavaScript 1.0

String objects can't be created explicitly in JavaScript 1.0. Any variable set to a quoted string is automatically a String object.

Strings can be created this way in all versions of JavaScript.

```
var s = "The quick brown fox ...";
// creates a String object set to "The quick brown fox ..."
var s = "";
// creates an empty string
```

String Methods and Properties

Following are descriptions of the methods and properties available in the String object to date.

anchor()

The `anchor()` method returns the value of a String object formatted as a named anchor using the `<A>` tag. It takes one argument, a string, which is used as the NAME attribute of the `<A>` tag.

`anchor()` is available in JavaScript 1.0 and higher.

```
var s = new String("Toyota");
var a = s.anchor("car");
  // a equals "<A NAME="car">Toyota</A>"
```

Note that this method prints HTML tags and attributes in uppercase. This is not compatible with any of the XHTML family of document types (XHTML 1.0, 1.1, or Basic), which is the current W3C HTML standard.

big()

The big() method returns the value of a String object formatted with the <BIG> tag. It takes no arguments.

big() is available in JavaScript 1.0 and higher.

```
var s = new String("Toyota");
var b = s.big();
// b equals "<BIG>Toyota</BIG>"
```

Note that this method prints HTML tags and attributes in uppercase. This is not compatible with any of the XHTML family of document types (XHTML 1.0, 1.1, or Basic), which is the current W3C HTML standard.

blink()

The blink() method returns the value of a String object formatted with the <BLINK> tag. It takes no arguments.

blink() is available in JavaScript 1.0 and higher.

```
var s = new String("Toyota");
var b = s.blink();
// b equals "<BLINK>Toyota</BLINK>"
```

Note that this method prints HTML tags and attributes in uppercase. This is not compatible with any of the XHTML family of document types (XHTML 1.0, 1.1, or Basic), which is the current W3C HTML standard. Additionally, the <BLINK> tag is only supported by Netscape.

bold()

The bold() method returns the value of a String object formatted with the <B> tag. It takes no arguments.

bold() is available in JavaScript 1.0 and higher.

```
var s = new String("Toyota");
var b = s.bold();
// b equals "<B>Toyota</B>"
```

Note that this method prints HTML tags and attributes in uppercase. This is not compatible with any of the XHTML family of document types (XHTML 1.0, 1.1, or Basic), which is the current W3C HTML standard.

charAt()

The charAt() method returns the character at a given position in a String object. It takes one argument, which is the index of the character to be returned. If the argument is a number smaller than zero or larger than the length of the string minus one, charAt() returns an empty string.

charAt() is available in JavaScript 1.2 and later, and was included in the ECMA-262 specification.

```
var s = new String("Toyota");
var c = s.charAt(4);
// c equals "t"
```

charCodeAt()

The charCodeAt() method returns the Unicode encoding of a character at a given position in a String object. It takes one argument, which is the index of the character whose code is to be returned.

charAt() is available in JavaScript 1.2 and later, and was included in the ECMA-262 specification. Early versions of Netscape 4 don't fully support all 65,535 values of the Unicode character set, but do match the first 128 characters of Unicode exactly.

```
var s = new String("Toyota");
var c = s.charAt(4);
// c equals "116"
```

concat()

The concat() method combines the values of two or more strings, appends them to the end of a String object, and returns the new string. It takes one or more arguments.

concat() is available in JavaScript 1.2 and later, and was included in the ECMA-262 specification.

```
var s = var s = new String("Toyota");
var c = s.concat(" is the name of my car.");
// c equals "Toyota is the name of my car."
```

This job can also be accomplished using the + operator.

fixed()

The `fixed()` method returns the value of a String object formatted using `<TT>` tags. It takes no arguments.

`fixed()` is available in JavaScript 1.0 and higher.

```
var s = new String("Toyota");
var f = s.fixed();
// f equals "<TT>Toyota</TT>"
```

Note that this method prints HTML tags and attributes in uppercase. This is not compatible with any of the XHTML family of document types (XHTML 1.0, 1.1, Basic), which is the current W3C HTML standard.

4

fontcolor()

The `fontcolor()` method returns the value of a String object formatted as a given color using the `<FONT>` tag. It takes one argument, a string, which should be an HTML-compatible font name or hexadecimal color.

`fontcolor()` is available in JavaScript 1.0 and higher.

```
var s = new String("Toyota");
var f = s.fontcolor("#0000FF");
// f equals "<FONT COLOR="#0000FF">Toyota</FONT>"
```

Note that this method prints HTML tags and attributes in uppercase. This is not compatible with XHTML, the current W3C HTML standard. Additionally, the `<FONT>` tag was deprecated in HTML 4 in favor of cascading style sheets.

fontsize()

The `fontsize()` method returns the value of a String object formatted as a given size using the `<FONT>` tag. It takes one argument, an integer between 1 and 7 or a string containing a relative size specification, such as "+1" or "-3."

`fontsize()` is available in JavaScript 1.0 and higher.

```
var s = new String("Toyota");
var f = s.fontsize(4);
// f equals "<FONT SIZE="6">Toyota</FONT>"
f = s.fontsize("-2");
// f equals "<FONT SIZE="-2">Toyota</FONT>"
```

Note that this method prints HTML tags and attributes in uppercase. This is not compatible with XHTML, the current W3C HTML standard. Additionally, the <FONT> tag was deprecated in HTML 4 in favor of cascading style sheets.

fromCharCode()

The fromCharCode() method creates and returns a string from character encodings. It takes one or more arguments that are 16-bit Unicode character values.

fromCharcode() is available in JavaScript 1.2 and later, and was included in the ECMA-262 specification. Early versions of Netscape 4 don't fully support all 65,535 values of the Unicode character set, but do match the first 128 characters of Unicode exactly.

```
var c = String.fromCharCode(84,111,121,111,116,97);
```

Note that fromCharCode() is a static method, so it must be referenced as String.fromCharCode() rather than a method of an instance of a String object.

indexOf()

The indexOf() method searches for a substring within a String object and returns the position index of its first occurrence of the substring. It takes two arguments. The first argument is the substring to search for, and the second argument, which is optional, is the index at which to start searching. The default is zero.

indexOf() returns the index representing the position where the substring begins. If the substring isn't found, indexOf() returns –1.

indexOf() is available in JavaScript 1.0 and higher, and was included in the ECMA-262 specification.

```
var s = new String("barbarella@webbedtogether.com");
var i = s.indexOf("b");
// i equals 0
var i2 = s.indexOf("b",1);
// i2 equals 3
var i2 = s.indexOf("z");
// i2 equals -1
```

italics()

The italics() method returns the value of a String object formatted with the <I> tag. It takes no arguments.

italics() is available in JavaScript 1.0 and higher.

```
var s = new String("Toyota");
var i = s.italics();
  // i equals "<I>Toyota</I>"
```

Note that this method prints HTML tags and attributes in uppercase. This is not compatible with any of the XHTML family of document types (XHTML 1.0, 1.1, Basic), which is the current W3C HTML standard.

lastIndexOf()

The lastIndexOf() method searches backward for a substring within a String object and returns the position index of its last occurrence of the substring. It takes two arguments. The first argument is the substring to search for; and the second argument, which is optional, is the index at which to start searching. The default is the end of the string, or the string's length minus one.

lastIndexOf() returns the index representing the position where the substring begins. If the substring isn't found, lastIndexOf() returns –1.

lastIndexOf() is available in JavaScript 1.0 and higher, and was included in the ECMA-262 specification.

```
var s = new String("barbarella@webbedtogether.com");
var i = s.lastIndexOf("b"); // i equals 3
var i2 = s.lastIndexOf("b",2); // i2 equals 0
var i2 = s.lastIndexOf("z"); // i2 equals -1
```

length

The length property of a String equals the number of characters in the string. length is read-only.

length is available in JavaScript 1.0 and higher, and was included in the ECMA-262 specification.

```
var s = new String("Toyota");
var i = s.length; // i equals 6
```

length can be used to process each character in a string. The following code creates a list of the Unicode character code for each character in a string.

```
var codes = "";
for(var i = 0; i < s.length; i++)
{
codes +=
    (s.charCodeAt(i) + ", "); }
// codes equals "84, 111, 121, 111, 116, 97,"
```

link()

The link() method returns the value of a String object formatted as a hyperlink using the <A> tag. It takes one argument, a string, which is used as the HREF attribute, or the URL to link to.

link() is available in JavaScript 1.0 and higher.

```
var s = new String("Toyota");
var a = s.link("http://www.toyota.com");
// a equals "<A HREF="http://www.toyota.com">Toyota</A>"
```

Note that this method prints HTML tags and attributes in uppercase. This is not compatible with any of the XHTML family of document types (XHTML 1.0, 1.1, Basic), which is the current W3C HTML standard.

match()

The match() method finds one or more regular expression matches within a String object and returns an array of the results of the test. It takes one or more arguments, each of which should be regular expressions. If no match is found, match() returns null. Otherwise, match() returns an array of the matched text.

match() is available in JavaScript 1.2 and higher, and was included in the third edition of the ECMA-262 specification.

```
var s = new String("barbarella@webbedtogether.com, Molly@YAHOO.COM");
var t = s.match(/.com/gi);
// t is an array containing [".com",".COM"]
```

To learn more about the large topic of regular expressions, see the "RegExp" section of this chapter.

replace()

The replace() method finds one or more regular expression matches within a String object and replaces each with a new string. It takes two arguments. The first argument should be a regular expression. The second argument is simply a string to replace everything matched with the first argument. If no match is found, match() returns null.

replace() is available in JavaScript 1.2 and higher, and was included in the third edition of the ECMA-262 specification.

```
var s = new String("barbarella@webbedtogether, Molly@YAHOO.COM");
var t = s.replace(/.com/gi, ".com");
// t now equals "barbarella@hotmail.com, Molly@YAHOO.com"
// Both instances of .com are lowercase.
```

`replace()` includes a special set of parameters that can be specified in its replacement text, as listed here:

Parameter	Replacement
`$$`	A dollar sign
`$&`	The matched substring
`$'`	The part of the string that preceded the matched substring
`` $` ``	The part of the string that followed the matched substring
`$1` through `$9`	The parenthesized subexpression within the regular expression that was used to match the substring

To learn more about the large topic of regular expressions, see the "RegExp" section of this chapter.

search()

The `search()` method performs a search for a regular expression and a String object. It takes one argument, which is a regular expression that will be searched for. `search()` returns the position where the substring that was matched begins, or –1 if no match was found.

`search()` is available in JavaScript 1.2 and higher, and was included in the third edition of the ECMA-262 specification.

```
var s = new String("barbarella@webbedtogether.com, Molly@YAHOO.COM");
var t = s.search(/.com/i);
// t now equals 18
t = s.search(/.net/i);
// t now equals -1
```

To learn more about the large topic of regular expressions, see the "RegExp" section of this chapter.

slice()

The `slice()` method extracts a portion of a string and returns a new string. It takes two arguments. The first argument is the position in the string where the slice should begin.

The `slice()` method extracts a portion of a String object and returns a new string. It takes two arguments. The first argument is the position where the slice should begin. If this number is negative, it indicates how many characters from the end of the string to begin.

The second argument is optional. It specifies the character position immediately after the last character that should be included in the slice. If this is left blank, the slice will end at the end of the string. If the position is after the end of the string, the selection will stop at the end of the string anyway. If this number is negative, it indicates how many array characters before the end of the string to end.

slice() is available in JavaScript 1.2 and higher, and was included in the ECMA-262 specification. In Internet Explorer 4 and 5, the first argument can't be a negative number.

```
var s = new String("barbarella@webbedtogether.com, Molly@YAHOO.COM");
var b = s.slice(0,22); // b equals "barbarella@webbedtogether.com
bar c = s.slice(-1,23);
```

small()

The small() method returns the value of a String object formatted with the <SMALL> tag. It takes no arguments.

small() is available in JavaScript 1.0 and higher.

```
var s = new String("Toyota");
var t = s.small();
// t equals "<SMALL>Toyota</SMALL>"
```

Note that this method prints HTML tags and attributes in uppercase. This is not compatible with any of the XHTML family of document types (XHTML 1.0, 1.1, Basic), which is the current W3C HTML standard.

split()

The split() method divides a String object into an array of substrings. It takes one argument, which is a delimiter by which the string should be divided. If this argument is left blank, split() returns an array with one element, which is the original string.

split() is available in JavaScript 1.1 and higher, and was included in the ECMA-262 specification. split() was enhanced in JavaScript 1.2 to also support regular expressions as a delimiter.

```
var s = new String("barbarella@webbedtogether.com,Molly@YAHOO.COM");
var a = s.split(", ");
// a is an array containing ["barbarella@webbedtogether.com",
   "Molly@YAHOO.COM"]
```

To learn more about the large topic of regular expressions, see the "RegExp" section of this chapter.

strike()

The `strike()` method returns the value of a String object formatted with the `<STRIKE>` tag. It takes no arguments.

`big()` is available in JavaScript 1.0 and higher.

```
var s = new String("Toyota");
var t = s.strike();
// t equals "<STRIKE>Toyota</STRIKE>"
```

Note that this method prints HTML tags and attributes in uppercase. This is not compatible with any of the XHTML family of document types (XHTML 1.0, 1.1, Basic), which is the current W3C HTML standard. Additionally, the `<STRIKE>` tag was deprecated in HTML 4.

sub()

The `sub()` method returns the value of a String object formatted with the `<SUB>` tag. It takes no arguments.

`sub()` is available in JavaScript 1.0 and higher.

```
var s = new String("Toyota");
var b = s.sub();
// b equals "<SUB>Toyota</SUB>"
```

Note that this method prints HTML tags and attributes in uppercase. This is not compatible with any of the XHTML family of document types (XHTML 1.0, 1.1, Basic), which is the current W3C HTML standard.

substr()

The `substr()` method extracts a portion of a string and returns it. `substr()` takes two arguments. The first argument is the character position where the substring should begin. This can be either a character position within the array, or a number indicating the position to start relative to the end of an array. To indicate a number relative to the end of an array, a negative number is used. For example, −1 indicates the last position in the string, −2 indicates the character before the last one in the string, and so on.

4

The second argument is a number indicating how many character positions until the end of the substring. If this parameter isn't included, `substr()` includes all characters until the end of the string.

`substr()` is available in JavaScript 1.2 and later, and is included in the ECMA-262 specification. In Internet Explorer 4 and 5, the first argument can't be a negative number.

```
var s = new String("Toyota");
var t = s.substr(0,3);
// t equals "Toy"
```

substring()

The `substring()` method extracts a portion of a string and returns it. `substring()` takes two arguments, which are two character positions within a string.

The first argument is the character position where the substring should begin. The second argument is a character position immediately following the ending character position.

Both arguments must be numbers between zero and the length of the array minus one, and the first argument must be smaller than the second one.

`substring()` is available in JavaScript 1.0 and later, and is included in the ECMA-262 specification.

```
var s = new String("Toyota");
var t = s.substring(0,3);
// t equals "Toy"
```

sup()

The `sup()` method returns the value of a String object formatted with the `<SUP>` tag. It takes no arguments.

`sup()` is available in JavaScript 1.0 and higher.

```
var s = new String("Toyota");
var b = s.sup();
// b equals "<SUP>Toyota</SUP>"
```

Note that this method prints HTML tags and attributes in uppercase. This is not compatible with any of the XHTML family of document types (XHTML 1.0, 1.1, Basic), which is the current W3C HTML standard.

toLowerCase()

The `toLowerCase()` method converts the value of a String object to lowercase letters.

`toLowerCase()` is available in JavaScript 1.0 and later, and was included in the ECMA-262 specification.

```
var s = new String("Toyota");
var l = s.toLowerCase();
// l equals "toyota"
```

toUpperCase()

The `toUpperCase()` method converts the value of a String object to uppercase letters.

`toUpperCase()` is available in JavaScript 1.0 and later, and was included in the ECMA-262 specification.

```
var s = new String("Toyota");
var u = s.toUpperCase();
// u equals "TOYOTA"
```

4

Chapter 5
JavaScript in the Browser: Client-Side Objects, Methods, and Properties

Embedding JavaScript in HTML Pages

You can embed JavaScript into HTML several different ways. This part of the chapter will go over each way and include examples.

`<SCRIPT>` Tags

The `<SCRIPT>` tags are the most common method of embedding JavaScript. They are used like most other HTML tags: start with a `<SCRIPT>` tag, insert any number of statements, and then end with a `</SCRIPT>` tag. The `<SCRIPT>` tags may be placed either in the `<HEAD>` or `<BODY>` of your HTML. An HTML document may contain any number of `<SCRIPT>` tags. Also, these tags are case insensitive.

```
<html><head><title>JavaScript Example</title>
<script type="text/javascript">
<!--//
function add_numbers(x,y) {
  var sum = x+y;
  document.write(sum);
  }
//-->
</script>
</head>
<body>
The sum of the numbers 20 and 35 is:
<script type="text/javascript">
<!--//
  add_numbers(20,35);
//-->
```

```
</script>
</body></html>
```

Notice in the preceding example, there are some odd-looking comment tags: `<!--//` and `//-->`. These comment tags are used for browsers that do not support JavaScript. If the tags are not used, the browser will display everything between the `<SCRIPT>` tags.

`<SCRIPT>` Tag Attributes

The `<SCRIPT>` tags optionally use several attributes that extend the functionality of the tag.

TYPE   This attribute is optional, but it is good practice to include it. The `TYPE` value defines the MIME type of the script that is enclosed in the `<SCRIPT>` tags. The following table lists the values for common MIME types:

MIME Type	Description
text/ecmascript	ECMA Script
text/javascript	JavaScript
text/jscript	Microsoft-specific JavaScript
text/vbscript	Visual Basic Script (VBScript)
text/vbs	Visual Basic Script (VBScript)
text/xml	XML

SRC   This optional attribute is used to embed an external JavaScript file. External JavaScript files should have the extension `.js`. This is a convenient way to clean up your HTML, especially if you need to use the same JavaScript in many pages.

```
<script src="/scripts/rollover.js"></script>
```

This example includes the `rollover.js` script, which resides in the `/scripts/` directory, in the current HTML document.

CHARSET   This is also an optional attribute, used with the SRC attribute. CHARSET means "character set," which is a set of written or computer language characters. The default CHARSET is ISO-8859-1. Other examples are SHIFT_JIS, UTF-8, PC8-Danish-Norwegian, and UNICODE-1-1.

A list of all character sets is available from the Internet Assigned Numbers Authority (IANA), at http://www.iana.org/assignments/character-sets.

DEFER   This attribute is a boolean value, which is used to make the browser wait until the entire page has loaded, before parsing the said script. Values are either TRUE, which makes the browser wait, or FALSE, which parses the script while the page is loading.

ARCHIVE   This attribute is used to embed JAR files, which may contain an archive of JavaScript files and/or digitally signed JavaScript files, for security.

```
<script archive="scripts.jar"></script>
```

LANGUAGE   This attribute is deprecated in favor of the TYPE attribute. Originally, it was used to define what kind of scripting language would be enclosed in the <SCRIPT> tags; for instance,

```
<!-- JavaScript -->
<script language="JavaScript">
<!-- Specifically JavaScript 1.1 -->
<script language="JavaScript1.1">
<!-- Microsoft VBScript -->
<script language="VBScript">
```

URL

Another way to execute JavaScript is in the URL. Rather than typing **http://**, you need to use **javascript:**. This is followed by one or more statements, for instance,

```
javascript:document.write
("This<br>contains<br>several<br>lines.")
```

By itself, it does not look particularly useful; but when used with an HREF, it becomes much more interesting:

```
<a href="javascript:MyFunction();
        ">Execute MyFunction</a>
```

You can also use this with an event handler, such as onClick or onMouseOver, to execute JavaScript when an event is performed. For example, you can execute a function when the mouse moves over a link:

```
<a href="javascript:;"
        onMouseover="javascript:MyFunction">link</a>
```

Notice in the HREF, the javascript: is followed by a semicolon, which tells the browser to do nothing when the link is clicked.

More precisely it means execute no statements. This may be used instead of a pound (#) symbol, to keep the browser from moving to the top of the document.

JSS

The Navigator 4 series of browsers introduced JavaScript Style Sheet Syntax, or JSS for short. JSS allows you to create style sheets using the properties of tags, classes, and ID attributes. JSS is not supported by Internet Explorer and will probably not be used in future versions. Like normal CSS, JSS should appear only in the header of a document. Here's an example:

```
<style type="text/javascript">
  tags.p.fontstyle="italic";
  tags.p.color="blue";
</style>
```

Entities

Another feature that is only available in the Navigator browsers, versions 3 and greater, is JavaScript Entities, which allow you to use a special sequence of characters to execute JavaScript statements. The entity begins with &{, followed by any JavaScript statements, which are divided by semicolons, and ends with };, for example,

```
<html><head>
<title>Test</title>
<script language="javascript">
  var MyColor="#aabbcc";
</script>
</head>
<body bgcolor="&{MyColor;};">
<p>TEST</p>
</body>
</html>
```

This example displays a page with a light blue background. Strangely, in Internet Explorer it displays a green background—in fact, every color displays a green background.

The Document Object Model

The Document Object Model (DOM) refers to the area of the web page inside the window. By using the DOM you may access all the objects within the web page, such as images, form elements, and the status bar.

The navigator Object

5

The navigator property contains read-only information about the user's system. This information includes the web browser, operating system, language, plug-ins, and MIME types. The navigator property may be used in either Netscape or Internet Explorer, though IE does have its own version called clientInformation, which returns the same information but is not available to Netscape. Table 5-1 lists the properties and functions of the navigator object.

Property	Description	JavaScript Version	Notes
appCodeName	Contains the code name of the browser	JavaScript 1.0	Read-only
appMinorVersion	Contains information about operating system updates	JavaScript 1.2	Read-only IE 5+ only
appName	Contains the name of the browser	JavaScript 1.0	Read-only
appVersion	Contains the version of the browser	JavaScript 1.0	Read-only

Table 5-1. navigator Properties and Functions

Property	Description	JavaScript Version	Notes
`cookieEnabled`	Contains a boolean value, which determines whether the user has cookies enabled	JavaScript 1.2	Read-only IE 5+ and Netscape 6+ only
`cpuClass`	Contains the type of CPU the user has	JavaScript 1.2	Read-only IE 5+ only
`javaEnabled()`	Tests the availability of Java	JavaScript 1.1	
`language`	Contains the default language of the browser	JavaScript 1.0	Read-only Netscape 4+ only
`mimeTypes[]`	An array containing the Mime types supported by the browser	JavaScript 1.1	Netscape only
`online`	Contains a boolean value, which determines whether the user is online or offline	JavaScript 1.2	Read-only IE 4+ only
`oscpu`	Displays the platform (operating system) that the browser is on	JavaScript 1.2	Read-only Netscape 6+ only
`platform`	Contains the platform (operating system) that the browser is on	JavaScript 1.2	Read-only

Table 5-1. `navigator` Properties and Functions *(continued)*

Property	Description	JavaScript Version	Notes
plugins[]	An array containing a list of installed plug-ins in the browser	JavaScript 1.1	Netscape only
product	Contains the product name for the browser	JavaScript 1.2	Read-only Netscape 6+ only
productSub	Contains version information about the product	JavaScript 1.2	Read-only Netscape 6+ only
systemLanguage	Contains the language of the platform	JavaScript 1.0	Read-only Internet Explorer only
userAgent	Contains the user-agent header in HTTP requests	JavaScript 1.0	Read-only
userLanguage	Contains the language of the browser	JavaScript 1.0	Read-only IE 4+ only
vendor	Contains browser vendor information	JavaScript 1.2	Read-only Netscape 6+ only
vendorSub	Contains version information about the vendor	JavaScript 1.2	Read-only Netscape 6+ only

Table 5-1.   navigator Properties and Functions *(continued)*

navigator.appCodeName

The appCodeName property is a read-only string that contains the code name of the browser.

```
document.write(navigator.appCodeName);
```

Versions of Netscape 2+, as well as Internet Explorer versions 3+, return Mozilla.

navigator.appMinorVersion

The `appMinorVersion` property is a string value, that returns browser and system upgrade information. It is only available for Internet Explorer 5+ browsers.

```
document.write(navigator.appMinorVersion);
//Returns: ;SP1;Q279328;
```

Each upgrade in the return is separated by a semicolon. As you can see, I have the Service Pack 1 upgrade and service alert Q279328.

navigator.appName

The `appName` is a read-only property, that returns the name of the application, the browser name.

```
document.write(navigator.appName);
//IE Returns: Microsoft Internet Explorer
//Netscape Returns: Netscape
```

navigator.appVersion

The `appVersion` property returns a read-only string, that contains information about the user's browser version, platform, language, encryption, and other details. The encryption is either U or I. U means U.S. release with high encryption; I means international release with standard encryption. Table 5-2 gives some examples.

navigator.cookieEnabled

The `cookieEnabled` property contains a boolean value, which determines whether or not the user has cookies enabled. The `navigator.cookieEnabled` property is available in IE 5+ and Netscape 6+.

```
document.write(navigator.cookieEnabled);
//Returns: true or false.
```

Example	Description
`4.0 (compatible; MSIE 4.01; Windows 98)`	Internet Explorer 4.01 on Windows 98
`4.04 [en] (Win95; I)`	English Netscape 4.04 on Windows 95, standard encryption
`4.05 [fr] (Win95; I)`	French Netscape 4.05 on Windows 95, standard encryption
`4.0 (compatible; MSIE 4.01; AOL 4.0; Windows 95)`	Internet Explorer 4.0 on Windows 95, using AOL 4.0
`4.05 [en] (X11; I; IRIX 6.3 IP32)`	English Netscape 4.05 on IRIX 6.3 running X-Windows (IRIX runs on SGI machines)
`3.04Gold (Win95; I)`	Netscape 3.04 Gold on Windows 95, standard encryption
`3.01 (X11; U; SunOS 4.1.4 sun4m)`	Netscape 3.01 on SunOS 4.1.4 running X-Windows
`4.01 (Macintosh; I; PPC)`	Netscape 4.01 on Macintosh Power PC, standard encryption
`3.0 (Win16; U)`	Netscape 3.0 on Windows 3.x, strong encryption
`3.01 DT [de]C-DT (Win95; I)`	German Netscape 3.01 on Windows 95, standard encryption
`Lynx 2.5 libwww-FM/2.14`	Lynx 2.5 text-only browser, probably on Linux
`4.05 [en] (X11; I; Linux 2.0.35 i586)`	English Netscape 4.05 on Linux 2.0.35 running X-Windows, standard encryption
`4.77 [en] (Windows NT 5.0; U)`	English Netscape 4.77 on Windows 2000, high encryption

Table 5-2.   Examples of `appVersion`

navigator.cpuClass

The `cpuClass` property contains a read-only value, that contains the processor type of the client. This property is only available for IE 5+.

```
document.write(navigator.cpuClass);
//Returns x86 which tells you that I am using an
//Intel or compatible CPU.
```

navigator.javaEnabled()

The javaEnabled() method determines whether Java is enabled in the browser, allowing you to display applets. It returns a boolean value of true or false.

```
document.write(navigator.javaEnabled());
```

navigator.language

The language property is a read-only property that returns the default language for the browser. It is only available for Netscape.

```
document.write(navigator.language);
```

This returns en for English, fr for French, jp for Japanese, and so on.

navigator.mimeTypes[]

The mimeTypes[] array contains each MIME type supported by the browser. You may refer to either the number of the MIME type in the array or the actual MIME type, enclosed in quotes. This is a Netscape-only property.

```
document.write(navigator.mimeTypes["image/x-quicktime"]);
document.write(navigator.mimeTypes[9]);
//Both return: [object MimeType]
```

If the returned data is [object MimeType], the specified MIME type is supported by the browser. If undefined is returned, the specified MIME type is not supported by the browser.

navigator.mimeTypes.length
The mimeTypes.length property returns the number of supported MIME types.

```
document.write(navigator.mimeTypes.length);
//My Browser Returns: 530
```

As you can see, my browser supports 530 different MIME types.

navigator.mimeTypes[].description
The mimeTypes[].description array displays a description of the requested MIME type.

```
document.write(navigator.mimeTypes
    ["image/x-quicktime"].description);
//This returns: QuickTime Image File
```

navigator.mimeTypes[].enabledPlugin

The mimeTypes[].enabledPlugin array determines whether a particular plug-in is enabled by the browser.

```
document.write(navigator.mimeTypes
    ["image/x-quicktime"].enabledPlugin);
//Returns: [object Plugin]
document.write(navigator.mimeTypes
    ["image/pcx"].enabledPlugin);
//Returns: null
```

5

The first example returns [object Plugin], which means that a plug-in for QuickTime is enabled. The second example returns nothing, which means that I do not have a plug-in enabled to handle PCX files.

navigator.mimeTypes[].suffixes

The mimeTypes[].suffixes array displays the file extensions, which are associated with a particular MIME type.

```
document.write(navigator.mimeTypes
["image/x-quicktime"].suffixes);
//Returns: qtif, qti
document.write(navigator.mimeTypes[33].suffixes[1]);
//Returns: wme, xml, xsl
document.write(navigator.mimeTypes["image/pcx"].suffixes);
//Returns: null
```

The first two examples return their associated extensions, while the last example returns null, because it is not supported.

navigator.mimeType[].type

The mimeType[].type array is used to identify the MIME type by the array element.

```
document.write(navigator.mimeTypes[2].type);
//Returns: image/x-targa
document.write(navigator.mimeTypes[33].type);
//Returns: text/xml
```

navigator.online

The online read-only boolean property determines whether the user's browser is in online mode. It is available in IE 5+ only.

```
document.write(navigator.onLine);
//Returns: true or false
```

navigator.oscpu

The oscpu read-only property returns the browser's platform system information. It is only available in Netscape 6+.

```
document.write(navigator.oscpu);
//Returns: Windows NT 5.0
```

navigator.platform

The platform property is another read-only property, which contains the platform (operating system) of the user.

```
document.write(navigator.platform);
```

This will vary between computers. Here are some examples:

Example	Description
Win32	32-bit version of Windows
Win16	16-bit version of Windows
MacPPC	Macintosh Power PC

navigator.plugins

The plugins object is only available in Netscape 3+. It is used to get information about which plug-ins users have installed on their system. A plug-in is a modular program that is used in conjunction with the web browser to support different types of embedded files. The plugins object is sometimes followed by an [n], where n is equal to the element number of the array; or it is equal to the name of the plug-in, which must be between single quotes.

```
document.write(navigator.plugins);
```

This returns [object PluginArray], which specifies that I have plugin support.

plugins[].description

The plugins[].description array contains a read-only string with the description of the specified plug-in.

```
document.write(navigator.plugins
['QuickTime Plug-in 5.0.2'].description);
document.write(navigator.plugins[3].description);
// Both return:
//The QuickTime Plugin allows you to view
//a wide variety of multimedia
//content in Web pages. For more information,
//visit the QuickTime Web site.
```

plugins[].filename

The plugins[].filename array contains the location of the file that controls the specified plug-in. The location is the location on the user's computer.

```
document.write(navigator.plugins
        ['QuickTime Plug-in 5.0.2'].filename);
document.write(navigator.plugins[3].filename);
// Both return:
// D:\Program Files\Netscape\Communicator\Program
// \plugins\npqtplugin4.dll
```

This example is the location of that file on my computer; it will vary from computer to computer, of course.

plugins[].length

The plugins[].length array contains the number of elements in the MimeType array.

```
document.write(navigator.plugins
        ['QuickTime Plug-in 5.0.2'].length);
document.write(navigator.plugins[3].length);
//Both return: 6
```

Both of the examples return 6; therefore, there are six MimeTypes for ShockWave Flash on my computer.

5

plugins[].name

The plugins[].name array contains the specific name of the plug-in, which is good for testing for plug-ins.

```
if (navigator.plugins
['QuickTime Plug-in 5.0.2'].name) {
  document.write("QuickTime Installed");
}
else {
  document.write("Please Install
          the QuickTime Plugin")
}
```

Here, if the user has the QuickTime plug-in, QuickTime Installed is displayed; if not, Please Install the QuickTime Plugin is displayed.

navigator.product

The product read-only array returns product information about the browser—specifically, whether the browser is using the Gecko engine. It is available in Netscape 6+ only.

```
document.write(navigator.product);
//Returns: Gecko
```

navigator.productSub

The productSub read-only property returns information about the release date of the navigator.product property. It is available in Netscape 6+ only. The format of the returned data is YYYYMMDD.

```
document.write(navigator.productSub);
//Returns: 20010131
```

navigator.systemLanguage

The systemLanguage property is read-only and only available for Internet Explorer 4+. It contains the language of the platform.

```
document.write(navigator.systemLanguage);
//Returns: en-us
```

navigator.userAgent

The userAgent property is read-only. It contains the navigator.appCodeName followed by a slash (/) and navigator.appVersion.

```
document.write(navigator.userAgent);
//IE Returns: Mozilla/4.0 (compatible; MSIE 5.01; Windows NT 5.0)
//Netscape Returns: Mozilla/4.77 [en] (Windows NT 5.0; U)
```

navigator.userLanguage

The userLanguage contains a read-only string, which describes the language of the user. It is only available in IE 4+.

```
document.write(navigator.userLanguage);
//Returns: en-us
```

navigator.vendor

The vendor read-only property contains information about the vendor of the browser. It is only available in Netscape 6+.

```
document.write(navigator.vendor);
//Returns: Netscape6
```

navigator.vendorSub

The vendorSub read-only property contains information about the version of the web browser. It is only available in Netscape 6+.

```
document.write(navigator.vendorSub);
//Returns: 6.01
```

The Event Object (Events and Event Handling)

Event describes details about an event. Events are handled by browsers in different ways.

Netscape 4 supports event handler arguments, which are coded as follows:

```
function handler(event) { ... }
```

Netscape 6 supports event listening, which is coded as follows:

```
object.adEventListner(eventType, functionCall, downBool)
```

Internet Explorer 4+ uses a window property, which is coded as follows:

```
window.event
```

Table 5-3 describes the events that are available for each browser.

event.altKey, event.ctrlKey, and event.shiftKey

The altKey, ctrlKey, shiftKey properties return a boolean value that determines whether or not the ALT, CTRL, or SHIFT keys were held down during an event.

Navigator 4	Netscape 6	Internet Explorer 4+
data	altKey, ctrlKey, shiftKey	altKey, ctrlKey, shiftKey
height	bubbles	button
layerX, layerY	button	cancelBubble
modifiers	cancelable	clientX, clientY
pageX, pageY	cancelBubble	fromElement
screenX, screenY	currentTarget	keyCode
target	eventPhase	offsetX, offsetY
type	keyCode	reason
TYPE	target	returnValue
which	type	screenX, screenY
width		srcElement
x, y		srcFilter
		toElement
		type
		x, y

Table 5-3.   Web Browser Properties

event.bubbles

The bubbles property returns a boolean that determines whether the event did continue to bubble up the hierarchy or not.

event.button

The button property determines which mouse button triggered the event. It returns left, right, or middle.

event.cancelable

The cancelable property returns a boolean that determines whether the event is cancelable or not. Some events are not cancelable.

event.cancelBubble

The cancelBubble property returns a boolean that determines whether the event should continue to bubble up the hierarchy.

event.clientX, event.clientY

The clientX and clientY properties return the x and y coordinates relative to the web browser page, where the event occurred.

event.currentTarget

The currentTarget property returns the object where the event currently is. Its event listener intercepted the event.

event.data

The data is used when "dragdrop" events occur. It refers to an array of strings; each element in the array represents a URL of a dropped object.

event.eventPhase

The eventPhase property returns the current phase of the event. Returned values are

eventPhase Value	Description
0	Capture.
1	The event just hit the target object.
3	Bubbling.

event.fromElement

The fromElement property refers to the object that the mouse pointer is moving. It is used for mouse movement events.

event.height

The height property is set when *resize* events occur. It contains the new height of the resized object.

event.keyCode

The keyCode property is used during keyboard events. It specifies the Unicode character code generated by the key that was struck.

event.layerX, event.layerY

The layerX and layerY properties specify the x and y coordinates, relative to the enclosing layer, at which the event occurred.

event.modifiers

The modifiers property specifies which keyboard modifiers were held down during an event. The value returned is a bitmask consisting of the following values: Event.ALT_MASK, Event.CONTROL_MASK, Event.META_MASK, or Event.SHIFT_MASK.

event.offsetX, event.offsetY

The offsetX and offsetY properties contain the x and y coordinates at the event that occurred, within the coordinates of the event itself.

event.pageX, event.pageY

The pageX and pageY properties contain the x and y coordinates relative to the web browser page, where the event occurred. The coordinates are relative to the top-level page.

event.reason

The reason property is used with the datasetcomplete event. It returns a code that specifies the status of data transfer. The values are as follows:

reason Value	Description
0	Successful transfer
1	Transfer aborted
2	An error occurred during transfer

event.returnValue

The `returnValue` property may be set to `true` or `false`. If set, it takes precedence over the value actually returned by an event handler. Set this to `false` to cancel the default action of the source element on which the event occurred.

event.screenX, event.screenY

The `screenX` and `screenY` properties determine where, relative to the screen, an event occurred.

event.srcElement

The `srcElement` property refers to the Window, Document, or HTML Element object that generated the event.

event.srcFilter

The `srcFilter` property is used in `filterchange` events. It specifies the filter that changed.

event.target

The `target` property refers to the Window, Document, or HTML Element object that generated the event.

event.toElement

The `toElement` property is used in mouse movement events. It refers to the object into which the mouse pointer is moving.

event.type

The `type` property specifies the type of the current event. It returns a value such as `onMouseOver`, without the `on` prefix.

Event.TYPE

The Event class defines bitmask constants for each of the supported event types. They are passed to `captureEvents()` and `releaseEvents()`. The available constants are as follows:

Event.ABORT	Event.KEYDOWN	Event.MOUSEUP
Event.BLUR	Event.KEYPRESS	Event.MOVE
Event.CHANGE	Event.KEYUP	Event.RESET
Event.CLICK	Event.LOAD	Event.RESIZE
Event.DBLCLICK	Event.MOUSEDOWN	Event.SELECT
Event.DRAGDROP	Event.MOUSEMOVE	Event.SUBMIT
Event.ERROR	Event.MOUSEOUT	Event.UNLOAD
Event.FOCUS	Event.MOUSEOVER	

event.which

The `which` property contains keyboard and mouse button events. If the keyboard was pressed during an event, it returns the pressed key's character encoding. If a mouse button was pressed, it returns the following possible values:

which Value	Description
1	Left mouse button
2	Middle mouse button
3	Right mouse button

event.width

The `width` property is set when *resize* events occur. It contains the new width of the resized object.

event.x, event.y

The `x` and `y` properties specify the x and y coordinates at which the event took place. In Netscape 4+, `event.x` and `event.y` are the same as `event.layerX` and `event.layerY`, which specify the position relative to the containing layer (if any). In IE 4+, the property specifies the position relative to the innermost containing element that is dynamically positioned using CSS-P.

The `window` Object

The `window` object describes the web browser's window or a frame. This object was first introduced in JavaScript 1.0, and later enhanced in JavaScript 1.1 and 1.2. Table 5-4 lists the properties of the `window` object, and Table 5-5 lists the methods.

Property	Description	JavaScript Version	Notes
`_content`	Displays content of current window	JavaScript 1.3	Netscape 6 or later
`closed`	Returns a boolean value that specifies whether a window has been closed	JavaScript 1.1	Read-only
`crypto`	References the Crypto object	JavaScript 1.2	Read-only Netscape 4.04 or later
`defaultStatus`	Specifies the default message that appears in the status bar	JavaScript 1.0	
`dialogArguments`	Returns any arguments that were used when the referenced modal dialog window was created	JavaScript 1.2	IE 4 or later
`dialogHeight`	Refers to the height of the referenced modal dialog window	JavaScript 1.2	IE 4 or later
`dialogLeft`	Refers to the horizontal offset of the referenced modal dialog window	JavaScript 1.2	IE 4 or later

Table 5-4.   Window Properties

Property	Description	JavaScript Version	Notes
dialogTop	Refers to the vertical offset of the referenced modal dialog window	JavaScript 1.2	IE 4 or later
dialogWidth	Refers to the width of the referenced modal dialog window	JavaScript 1.2	IE 4 or later
document	Refers to the Document object contained in the window	JavaScript 1.0	Read-only
event	Contains details about the most recent event	JavaScript 1.2	Read-only IE 4or later
frames[]	An array referring to the frames in the window	JavaScript 1.0	Read-only
history	Refers to the History object for the window	JavaScript 1.0	Read-only
innerHeight	Specifies the height of the document		Netscape 6 or later
innerWidth	Specifies the width of the document		Netscape 6 or later
length	The number of elements of the frames[] array	JavaScript 1.0	Read-only Also frames. length
location	Refers to the Location object in the window	JavaScript 1.0	
locationbar	Specifies the visibility of the location bar	JavaScript 1.1	Netscape 4 or later
menubar	Specifies the visibility of the menu bar	JavaScript 1.1	Netscape 4 or later
name	Contains the name of the window	JavaScript 1.0	Read-only in JavaScript 1.0 Read/write in JavaScript 1.1
offscreen Buffering	Specifies the type of buffering performed by the browser	JavaScript 1.0	
onblur	Specifies when the window loses keyboard focus	JavaScript 1.1	

5

Table 5-4. Window Properties *(continued)*

Property	Description	JavaScript Version	Notes
ondragdrop	Invoked when the user uses drag and drop	JavaScript 1.1	Netscape 4+ only
onerror	Specifies when an error handler function is invoked	JavaScript 1.1	
onfocus	Specifies when the window gains keyboard focus	JavaScript 1.1	
onload	Specifies when the document or frameset loads	JavaScript 1.0	
onmove	Specifies when the user moves a top-level window	JavaScript 1.1	Netscape 4 or later Not supported on Unix platforms
onresize	Specifies when a user resizes a window or frame	JavaScript 1.2	
onunload	Specifies when the user unloads a window or frameset	JavaScript 1.0	
opener	Refers to the Window object that called open() to create the current window	JavaScript 1.1	Read-only in Netscape Read/write in IE
outerHeight	Returns the window's total height	JavaScript 1.2	Netscape 4 or later
outerWidth	Returns the window's total width	JavaScript 1.2	Netscape 4 or later
pageXOffset	Returns the difference between the current horizontal position in the page and the page's leftmost edge	JavaScript 1.2	Netscape 4 or later
pageYOffset	The difference between the current vertical position in the page and the page's topmost edge	JavaScript 1.2	Netscape 4 or later

Table 5-4. Window Properties *(continued)*

Property	Description	JavaScript Version	Notes
parent	Refers to the parent window or frame of the current window	JavaScript 1.0	Read-only Only used when the current window is a frame
personalbar	Shows or hides the personal bar	JavaScript 1.1	Read-only Netscape 4 or later
screen	Refers to the Screen object of the window	JavaScript 1.0	Read-only
screenX	Specifies the x coordinate of the upper-left corner of the window	JavaScript 1.1	Netscape 4 or later
screenY	Specifies the y coordinate of the upper-left corner of the window	JavaScript 1.1	Netscape 4 or later
scrollbars	Specifies the visibility of the scroll bars	JavaScript 1.1	Read-only Netscape 4 or later
self	Refers to the window itself	JavaScript 1.0	Read/write in Netscape Read-only in IE Also window
sidebar	Specifies the visibility of the side	JavaScript 1.2	Read-only Netscape 6 or later
status	Refers to the current contents of the status line	JavaScript 1.0	Read/write
statusbar	Specifies the visibility of the status bar	JavaScript 1.1	Netscape 4 or later
toolbar	Specifies the visibility of the toolbar	JavaScript 1.1	Netscape 4 or later
top	Returns the window object of the topmost browser	JavaScript 1.0	Read-only
window	window.window is the same as window		Read-only

Table 5-4.   Window Properties *(continued)*

Method	Description	JavaScript Version	Notes
alert()	Makes an alert box	JavaScript 1.0	
atob()	Decodes a Base-64 encoded string	JavaScript 1.1	Netscape 4.x only Does not work in Netscape 6+
back()	URL of the previous page	JavaScript 1.1	Netscape 4+ only
blur()	Removes keyboard focus	JavaScript 1.1	
btoa()	Encodes data to Base-64	JavaScript 1.1	
captureEvents()	Allows you to capture some events	JavaScript 1.1	Netscape 4+ only
clearInterval()	Cancels a corresponding setInterval method	JavaScript 1.2	
clearTimeout()	Clears a specified timeout	JavaScript 1.2	
close()	Closes a top-level browser	JavaScript 1.0	
confirm()	Returns an OK or CANCEL dialog box	JavaScript 1.0	
disableExternalCapture()	Disallows a signed script to capture events in pages	JavaScript 1.2	Netscape 4+ only
enableExternalCapture()	Allows a signed script to capture events in pages	JavaScript 1.2	Netscape 4+ only
escape()	Converts ASCII characters to HEX characters	JavaScript 1.2	
execScript()	Allows you to execute a script in a certain language	JavaScript 1.2	IE 4+ only

Table 5-5. Window Methods

Method	Description	JavaScript Version	Notes
find()	Allows you to find in the current document	JavaScript 1.2	Netscape 4+ only
focus()	Gives the current window keyboard focus	JavaScript 1.1	
forward()	Returns the next document in the browser's history	JavaScript 1.1	Netscape 4+ only
home()	Sends users to their home URL	JavaScript 1.1	Netscape 4+ only
moveBy()	Moves the window to a relative position	JavaScript 1.2	
moveTo()	Moves the window to an absolute position	JavaScript 1.2	
navigate()	Sends the browser to a new URL	JavaScript 1.0	IE 3 or later
open()	Opens a new browser window	JavaScript 1.0, enhanced in JavaScript 1.1	
print()	Prints the document	JavaScript 1.1	Netscape 4+
prompt()	Gets a string for input	JavaScript 1.0	
releaseEvents()	Used to release events that had previously been captured	JavaScript 1.1	Netscape 4+ only
resizeBy()	Resizes the window	JavaScript 1.2	
resizeTo()	Used to resize the window to a specific size	JavaScript 1.2	
routeEvents()	Used to route an event that has been previously captured	JavaScript 1.2	Netscape 4+

5

Table 5-5.   Window Methods *(continued)*

Method	Description	JavaScript Version	Notes
scroll()	Used to automatically move the user to any point in the current window	JavaScript 1.1	Netscape 6 or later
scrollBy()	Scrolls the viewing area of the window by the amounts specified in the values	JavaScript 1.2	
scrollTo()	Scrolls the viewing window to an exact pixel position	JavaScript 1.2	
setHotkeys()	Allows or disallows use of keyboard shortcuts	JavaScript 1.2	
setInterval()	Used to either call a JavaScript function, or evaluate an expression	JavaScript 1.2	Netscape 4 or later Partial support for IE 4+
setResizable()	Allows or disallows window resizing	JavaScript 1.2	
setTimeout()	Pauses the execution of JavaScript	JavaScript 1.0	
setZOptions()	Controls window stacking	JavaScript 1.2	
showModalDialog()	Creates a modal dialog box that displays the document	JavaScript 1.2	IE 4or later
showModeless Dialog()	Creates a modeless dialog box that displays the document	JavaScript 1.3	IE 5 or later
stop()	Stops loading a document	JavaScript 1.1	
unescape()	Converts HEX characters to ASCII characters	JavaScript 1.2	

Table 5-5. Window Methods *(continued)*

window._content

The _content property is used to display the contents of the current window.

```
// if your URL is:
// http://www.mcgraw-hill.com
   /index.html
document.write(window._content.location.host);
//This prints: www.mcgraw-hill.com
```

window.alert()

The alert() method is used to display a user dialog box. The dialog box contains text, which you supply, and an OK button. The syntax of this method is as follows:

```
window.alert("message");
```

window.atob() and window.btoa()

The atob() and btoa() methods, respectively, decode and encode base-64 strings and return the results as a string.

```
var encode = btoa("encode this text") var decode =
window.atob("ZGVjb2RlIHRoaXMgdGV4dA==");
document.write(encode);
document.write(decode);
```

This returns the encoded string ZW5jb2RlIHRoaXMgdGV4dA==, followed by the decoded string decode this text. Note that I did not pass atob() the same btoa() encoded string.

window.back()

The back() method returns a string containing the URL of previously visited pages.

window.blur()

The blur() method removes the keyboard focus from the top-level browser window specified in the Window object.

5

window.captureEvents()

The captureEvents() event can be used to set the Window (or Document) object to handle single or various events that would otherwise be handled by different document elements. For example,

```
window.captureEvents( Event.Click | Event.DblClick)
```

The example sets up the window to capture all click and double-click events (onclick and ondblclick). Once a window has captured events, you then need to decide what happens with them. The various options are as follows:

Option	Description
Return true	Whatever element received the event that was captured by the window event will perform its default action. (For example, an <A> element's default action is to navigate to the URL provided in its HREF attribute.)
Return false	The default action of the element receiving the event will not occur. (For example, the link will not navigate to the URL.)
Call routeEvent method	This causes JavaScript to search for other event handlers for the event. For example, the Document object may have been trying to capture the event. Failing another object trying to capture the event, JavaScript will look to the original intended target of the event, in order to decide what to do.
Call the handleEvent method	This will force another element/object (that can handle such an event) to handle it, normally by performing its default action.

window.clearInterval()

The clearInterval() method cancels a corresponding setInterval method. The syntax is as follows:

```
window.clearInterval(MyInterval);
```

window.clearTimeout()

The clearTimeout() method is used to clear a specified setTimeout method, by referencing it by the ID of the setTimeout method. The syntax is as follows:

```
window.clearTimeout(MyTimeout);
```

window.close()

The close() method closes a top-level browser window.

window.closed

The closed property is a read-only boolean value that determines whether the window has been closed. Window objects that are closed do not simply disappear; their window.closed property is set to true.

window.confirm()

The confirm() method returns a dialog box, which prompts the user to press OK or CANCEL. There is also a definable message in the box. The syntax is as follows:

```
window.confirm("Question Here");
```

window.crypto

The crypto property is a reference to the Crypto object associated in the window. This property is for Netscape 4+ only.

window.dialogArguments

The dialogArguments property returns any arguments that were used when the referenced modal dialog window was created. Note that this property only applies to windows created with the showModalDialog method.

window.dialogHeight

The `dialogHeight` property refers to the height of the referenced modal dialog window. It is set as one of the features in the `showModalDialog` method.

window.dialogLeft

The `dialogLeft` property reflects the horizontal offset of the referenced modal dialog window, relative to the left edge of the desktop. It is set as one of the features in the `showModalDialog` method.

window.dialogTop

The `dialogTop` property refers to the vertical offset of the referenced modal dialog window, relative to the top edge of the desktop. It is set as one of the features in the `showModalDialog` method.

window.dialogWidth

The `dialogWidth` property refers to the width of the referenced modal dialog window. It is set as one of the features in the `showModalDialog` method.

window.disableExternalCapture()

The `disableExternalCapture()` method disallows the browser to accept information passed from different servers.

window.document

The `document` property contains the Document object for the referenced window. The Document object has properties that contain information about the current document being viewed in the browser window object, for instance,

```
myLinkColor=parent.document.linkColor
```

window.enableExternalCapture()

The enableExternalCapture() method allows the browser to accept information passed from different servers.

window.escape() and window.unescape()

The escape() and unescape() methods, respectively, convert ASCII characters to HEX characters, and vice versa. The HEX characters are returned in %xx format.

```
var escaped = window.escape("s+~!@#$%^&*()\n\t");
var unescaped = window.unescape(escaped);
document.write(escaped);
document.write("<BR>");
document.write(unescaped);
```

This first returns the string
s+%7E%21%40%23%24%25%5E%26*%28%29%0A%09,
which you can see is the encoded string. The second string returned is s+~!@#$%^&*(), which is the original string passed.

window.event

The event property contains details about the most recent event. In IE 4, no Event object is passed to an event handler, so the event handlers must obtain information about the event from the event property of the Window object.

window.execScript

The execScript method can be used to execute script functions in a certain language.

window.find()

The find method invokes the Find window of the browser, allowing the user to search for any text in the current document. Its effect is as if the user had chosen the Find command from the Edit menu.

window.focus()

The `focus()` method gives the keyboard focus to the window specified by the Window object.

window.forward()

The `forward()` method acts like the browser's forward button, moving the user to the next page, if available.

window.frames[]

The `frames[]` array contains a reference to any frames in the current window. You may refer to a frame by name or element number. You may also use the `length` property, as in `document.frames.length`.

window.history

The `history` property contains a read-only list of the browser's current history list (a list of recently visited sites).

window.home()

The `home()` method sends users to their *home* URL. This works in Netscape 4+ only.

window.innerHeight

The `innerHeight` property refers to the height, in pixels, of the document display area of `window`. This is not including menu bar, toolbars, and so on.

window.innerWidth

The `innerWidth` property refers to the width, in pixels, of the document display area of `window`. This is not including menu bar, toolbars, and so on.

window.length

The length property contains the number of frames contained in window, the default value is 0.

window.location

The location property refers to the Location object of window. It specifies the URL of the current document.

window.locationbar

The locationbar property allows you to hide or view the location bar. The syntax of this property is as follows:

```
window.locationbar.visibility
```

window.menubar

The menubar property allows you to hide or view the menu. The syntax of this property is as follows:

```
window.menubar.visibility
```

window.moveBy()

The moveBy() method can be used to reposition the Navigator window relative to its current position.

window.moveTo()

The moveTo() method can be used to move the Navigator window to a specific point on the screen, by moving the upper-left corner of the Navigator to the position specified.

window.name

The name property specifies the name of the window. If the window is not named, no value is returned.

window.navigate()

The `navigate()` method sends the browser to a new URL. This method works in IE 4+ only.

```
var newURL = window.navigate("http://www.mcgraw-hill.com");
document.write(newURL);
```

window.offscreenBuffering

The `offscreenBuffering` is set to a string value of `auto`, and it decides whether `offscreenbuffering` is necessary. This can be overridden in a script function, by explicitly setting the `offscreenBuffering` property to `true` or `false`. Once it has been set (either way), it returns a boolean value, representing whether `offscreenbuffering` is enabled or not.

window.onblur

The `onblur` property specifies an event handler function, which is invoked when the window loses keyboard focus.

window.ondragdrop

The `ondragdrop` property is invoked when the users use system drag-and-drop capabilities on an object or object on the window.

window.onerror

The `onerror` property is invoked when a JavaSript error occurs.

window.onfocus

The `onfocus` property is invoked when the window gains keyboard focus.

window.onload

The `onload` property is invoked when a document completes loading.

window.onmove

The onmove property is invoked when the window is moved.

window.onresize

The onresize property is invoked when the window is resized.

window.onunload

The onunload property is invoked when the window or frameset is unloaded for another page to be loaded in its place.

window.open()

The open() method opens a new browser window, using the following syntax:

```
window.open(url, name, features, replace)
```

The arguments are as follows:

Argument	Description
url	Specifies the URL to be displayed in the new window; if omitted, the new window will be blank.
name	An optional name for the new window, to allow you to use the TARGET attribute of the <A> tag.
features	Specifies which features of a web browser window are to appear in the new window.
replace	If set to true, the history of the window is cleared when a new document is loaded.

Window features should be set to true or false, depending on which ones you want to enable or disable. The syntax for features is as follows:

```
feature=value
```

Table 5-6 describes the features that may be used in the window.open method.

Feature	Description	Browser
alwaysLowered	Sends the window to the bottom of all the windows on the screen	Netscape 4+
alwaysRaised	Sends the window to the top of all the windows on the screen	Netscape 4+
channelmode	Specifies whether the window should appear in channel mode	IE 4+
dependent	Determines whether the window should be a child of the current window	Netscape 4+
directories	Directory buttons, like "What's Cool" and "What's New"	Netscape
fullscreen	Determines whether the browser should be in full-screen mode	IE 4+
height	Specifies the height in pixels of the document window	
hotkeys	Disables keyboard shortcuts	Netscape 4+
innerHeight	Specifies the height in pixels of the document display area	Netscape 4+
innerWidth	Specifies the width in pixels of the document display area	Netscape 4+
left	The x coordinate, in pixels, of the window	IE 4+
location	The URL bar	
menubar	The menu bar, which includes File, Edit, and so on.	
outerHeight	Specifies the total height in pixels of the window	Netscape 4+
outerWidth	Specifies the total width in pixels of the window	Netscape 4+
resizable	Allows the window to be resized	
screenX	The x coordinate, in pixels, of the window	Netscape 4+
screenY	The y coordinate, in pixels, of the window	Netscape 4+
scrollbars	Enables the horizontal and vertical scroll bars	
status	The status bar	
toolbar	The toolbar with the back and forward buttons	
top	The y coordinate, in pixels, of the window	IE4+

Table 5-6. Window Properties

Feature	Description	Browser
width	The width, in pixels, of the window's document display area	
z-lock	Specifies that the window should not be raised in stacking order	Netscape 4+

Table 5-6.   Window Features *(continued)*

window.opener

The opener property returns the name of the window that created the current window (via a window.open() event). It can be used with further object properties (such as location, and so on.) to access properties of the window/document that opened the current window, or methods (such as close()) to automatically close the window that created the current window.

window.outerHeight

The outerHeight property returns a value representing the referenced window's total height (including toolbars, scroll bars, and so on.), in pixels.

window.outerWidth

The outerWidth property returns a value representing the referenced window's total width (including toolbars, scroll bars, and so on.), in pixels.

window.parent

In a normal document window, the parent property refers to the page in the window. In a framed document, the parent property refers to the frameset document that the document is contained in.

window.personalbar

The personalbar property supports the personalbar property, which has a boolean property of visible. The syntax of this property is as follows:

```
window.personalbar.visible=false
```

window.print()

The print() method prints the current document, the same as the Print button.

window.prompt()

The prompt() method prompts the user for input. There are three buttons on this message box: OK, Clear, and Cancel. The syntax of this method is as follows:

```
window.prompt(message, default);
```

The buttons are explained here:

Button	Description	Returns
OK	Submits the data	The data, which the user entered
Clear	Clears the data	Nothing
Cancel	Cancels the input	null

window.releaseEvents()

The releaseEvents() method can be used to release events that had previously been captured using the captureEvents method. The syntax for releasing single or multiple events is the same as for the captureEvents method.

window.resizeBy()

The resizeBy() method resizes the window from its current size by the amounts specified. The syntax is as follows:

```
self.resizeBy(x,y)
```

window.resizeTo()

The resizeTo() method can be used to resize the window to a specific size. The syntax is as follows:

```
self.resizeTo(x,y)
```

window.routeEvents()

The routeEvents() method can be used to route an event that has been previously captured using the captureEvents method. The syntax is as follows:

```
objectReference.routeEvent(eventType)
```

window.screen

The screen property provides a reference to the Screen object, for obtaining properties of the user's current resolution, and so on.

window.screenX

The screenX property refers to the x coordinate of the upper-left corner of window on the screen. If the window is a frame, this property specifies the upper-left window that contains the frame.

window.screenY

The screenY property refers to the y coordinate of the upper-left corner of window on the screen. If the window is a frame, this property specifies the upper-left window that contains the frame.

window.scroll()

The scroll() method can be used to automatically move the user to any point in the current window. It is similar to midpage links, using <a href="#..."> constructs, except it moves the user to a position of pixel values, rather than links. The syntax of this method is as follows:

```
SomeWindow.scroll(x,y)
```

window.scrollbars

The scrollbars property supports the scrollbars property, which has a boolean property of visible. The syntax of this property is as follows:

```
window.scrollbars.visible=false
```

window.scrollBy()

The scrollBy() method scrolls the viewing area of the window by the amounts specified in the values. The syntax of this property is as follows:

```
self.scrollBy (x,y)
```

window.scrollTo()

The scrollTo() method scrolls the viewing window to an exact pixel position, given by the values. The syntax of this property is as follows:

```
self.scrollTo (x,y)
```

window.self

The window.self property contains a reference to the Window object specified by windows. This property is the same as window.

window.setHotkeys()

The setHotkeys() method allows you to enable or disable the user's use of keyboard shortcuts. It is available for windows without a menu bar only. The syntax of this method is as follows:

```
window.setHotkeys(boolean_value);
```

window.setInterval()

The setInterval() method allows JavaScript to execute a string continuously, at a set interval of milliseconds. The syntax of this method is as follows:

```
window.setInterval(string, interval);
window.setInterval(function, interval, arguments);
```

Here is an explanation of the arguments:

Argument	Description	Notes
string	Contains strings of JavaScript that should be executed at the interval; multiple strings should be separated by semicolons.	
function	A function to be executed at the interval.	Not available for IE
interval	The interval between each invocation of the function or string; interval time is in milliseconds.	
arguments	Arguments that are passed to the function.	

window.setResizable()

The setResizable() method allows you to enable or disable the user's ability to resize a window. The syntax of this property is as follows:

```
window.setResizable(boolean_value);
```

window.setTimeout()

The setTimeout() method allows you to delay the execution of a function or string. The syntax of this method is as follows:

```
window.setTimeout(string, delay);
```

The arguments are defined as follows:

Argument	Description
string	A string of JavaScript that you want to delay
delay	The time in milliseconds of the delay

window.setZOptions()

The setZOptions() method allows you to specify the stacking behavior of the windows. The syntax of this method is as follows:

```
window.setZOptions(option);
```

Here is an explanation of the options:

Option	Description
"alwaysRaised"	The window should always be on top.
"alwaysLowered"	The window should always be on the bottom.
"z-lock"	The window remains locked in the stacking order.
" "	When no option is passed, it acts like a normal window.

window.showHelp()

The `showHelp()` method displays a `.htm` or `.chm` help file. The syntax of this method is as follows:

```
window.showHelp(URL);
```

window.showModalDialog() and window.showModelessDialog()

The `showModalDialog()` and `showModelessDialog()` methods create a dialog box that displays a document.

The `showModalDialog()` dialog box is similar to an `alert()` type box, in that the user cannot change the focus from the dialog box back to the originating window. The `showModelessDialog()` dialog box is similar, but the user can still interact with the underlying window.

The syntax of these methods is the same, although they have slightly different uses:

```
window.showModalDialog(URL, arguments, features);
window.showModelessDialog(URL, arguments, features);
```

The arguments are as follows:

Argument	Description
URL	The URL that goes into the dialog box
arguments	Specifies the arguments to use in the dialog box
features	Specifies the features to use in the dialog box

Table 5-7 explains the features of window.showModalDialog()
and window.showModelessDialog().

window.sidebar

The sidebar property supports the sidebar property, which
has a boolean property of visible. The syntax of this property
is as follows:

```
window.sidebar.visible=false
```

Feature	Description	Values	Notes
dialogHeight	Sets the height of the dialog box; minimum of 100	Number of pixels	
dialogWidth	Sets the height of the dialog box	Number of pixels	
dialogLeft	Sets the x coordinate of the dialog box, relative to the upper-left corner of the screen	Position in pixels	
dialogTop	Sets the y coordinate of the dialog box, relative to the upper-left corner of the screen	Position in pixels	
center	Centers the dialog box on the desktop; default is yes	yes or no 1 or 0	
help	Specifies whether the dialog window displays the context-sensitive Help icon.	yes or no 1 or 0	
resizable	Specifies whether the dialog window has set dimensions; default for both dialog windows is no	yes or no 1 or 0	IE 5+ only
status	Specifies whether the dialog window displays a status bar; the default is yes	yes or no 1 or 0	IE 5+ only

Table 5-7.   showModalDialog() and showModelessDialog()
Features, Descriptions, and Values

5

window.status

The status property allows the status bar to be changed, for example,

```
self.status="New Status Bar Text"
```

window.statusbar

The statusbar property supports the statusbar property, which has a boolean property of visible. The syntax of this property is as follows:

```
window.statusbar.visible=false
```

window.stop()

The stop() method has the same functionality as the Stop button. It stops a window from loading.

window.toolbar

The toolbar property supports the toolbar property, which has a boolean property of visible. The syntax of this property is as follows:

```
window.toolbar.visible=false
```

window.top

The top property returns the window object of the topmost browser window.

window.window

The window property is the same as the window.self property.

window.XOffset

The XOffset property reflects the difference between the current horizontal position in the page and the page's leftmost edge. That is, as a page is scrolled horizontally, the `pageXOffset` will increase or decrease, being 0 if the current viewing area is the leftmost edge of the page. (Note that this is similar to Internet Explorer's scrollLeft property, but the two are incompatible.)

window.YOffset

The `YOffset` property reflects the difference between the current vertical position in the page and the page's uppermost edge. That is, as a page is scrolled vertically, the `pageYOffset` will increase or decrease, being 0 if the current viewing area is the uppermost edge of the page. (Note that this is similar to Internet Explorer's scrollTop property, but the two are incompatible.)

5

Document Properties

Document properties are either single properties or an array of properties. The property `anchors[]`, for example, refers to the Anchor objects in the document. These arrays, like normal arrays, begin with the number 0, which represents the first instance of the property. Table 5-8 describes the properties that the Document defines; Table 5-9 summarizes the functions.

Property	Description	JavaScript Version	Notes
activeElement	Returns the currently active element	JavaScript 1.2	IE 4+ only
alinkColor	Color of a link when the user is clicking on it; refers to the ALINK attribute of <BODY>	JavaScript 1.0	
all	Contains an array of all elements in the document	JavaScript 1.2	IE 4+ only
anchors[]	An array of the anchors in the document	JavaScript 1.2	

Table 5-8.   Document Properties and Descriptions

Property	Description	JavaScript Version	Notes
applets[]	An array of the applets in the document	JavaScript 1.1	
attributes	An unordered set of attribute information	JavaScript 1.3	Netscape 6+ only
bgColor	The background color of the document; refers to the BGCOLOR property of <BODY>	JavaScript 1.0	
body	Contains the entire content of the <BODY> element	JavaScript 1.2	Read/write in Netscape 6+ Read-only in IE 4+
characterSet	Contains the character set of the browser	JavaScript 1.3	Netscape 6+ only
childNodes	Contains information about each element in the document	JavaScript 1.2	Read/write in Netscape 6+ Read-only in IE 4+
cookie	Allows JavaScript to read and write HTTP cookies	JavaScript 1.0	
defaultCharset	Contains character information	JavaScript 1.2	IE 5.5+ only
documentElement	Contains root document information	JavaScript 1.3	Netscape 6+ only
domain	Allows trusted servers in the same domain to reduce certain security restrictions for interaction within their pages	JavaScript 1.1	
embeds[]	An array of the embedded objects in the document	JavaScript 1.1	
expando	Accepts a boolean value that determines whether or not arbitrary properties may be declared	JavaScript 1.2	Internet Explorer 4+ only

Table 5-8.   Document Properties and Descriptions *(continued)*

Property	Description	JavaScript Version	Notes
fgColor	The text color of the document; refers to the <TEXT> attribute of <BODY>	JavaScript 1.0	
fileCreatedDate	Date of file creation	JavaScript 1.2	IE 4+ only
fileModifiedDate	Date of file modification	JavaScript 1.2	IE 4+ only
fileSize	File's size	JavaScript 1.2	IE 4+ only
fileUpdatedDate	File's updated date	JavaScript 1.2	IE 4+ only
forms[]	An array of the form objects in the document	JavaScript 1.0	
frames[]	Contains an array of <IFRAME> tags	JavaScript 1.1	Netscape 6+ and IE 4+ only
height	Contains the height of the document	JavaScript 1.0	Netscape 4+
images[]	An array of the image objects in the document	JavaScript 1.1	
lastModified	The modification date of the document	JavaScript 1.0	
linkColor	The color of unvisited links in the document; refers to the LINK property of <BODY>	JavaScript 1.0	
links[]	An array that contains each link in the document	JavaScript 1.0	
location	Deprecated— same as URL		See URL
mimeType	Contains the MIME type of the current document	JavaScript 1.2	IE 5.5+ only
nameProp	Contains the title of the document	JavaScript 1.2	IE 5.5+ only
parentWindow	Returns a reference to the referenced document's parent window	JavaScript 1.2	IE 5.5+ only

Table 5-8.   Document Properties and Descriptions *(continued)*

5

Property	Description	JavaScript Version	Notes
readyState	Contains the loading status of a document	JavaScript 1.0	IE 4+ only
referrer	The last URL the user clicked, if any	JavaScript 1.0	
scripts[]	An array of every script in the document	JavaScript 1.2	IE 5.5+ only
selection	Contains a reference to selected content	JavaScript 1.2	IE 4+ only
styleSheets[]	An array of all style sheets in a document	JavaScript 1.2	IE 4+ and Netscape 6+ only
title	Contains the data between the <TITLE> and </TITLE> tags	JavaScript 1.0	
URL	The current URL	JavaScript 1.1	
vlinkColor	The color of visited links in the document; refers to the VLINK property of <BODY>	JavaScript 1.0	
width	Contains the width of the current document	JavaScript 1.0	Netscape 4+ only

Table 5-8.   Document Properties and Descriptions *(continued)*

Function	Description	JavaScript Version	Notes
clear()	Clears a document	JavaScript 1.0	Deprecated
close()	Closes the output to a document	JavaScript 1.0	
createElement()	Used to create <IMG> or <OPTION> elements	JavaScript 1.2	
create StyleSheet()	Used to create a style sheet	JavaScript 1.2	
elementFrom Point()	Determines the HTML element at a point	JavaScript 1.0	IE 4+ only

Table 5-9.   Document Functions and Descriptions

Function	Description	JavaScript Version	Notes
execCommand()	Used to execute commands in the document	JavaScript 1.0	IE 4+ only
getSelection()	Return the selected text	JavaScript 1.2	Netscape 4+ only
open()	Opens a text stream to a document	JavaScript 1.1	Netscape 4+ only
queryCommand Enabled()	Determines whether a specific command is available	JavaScript 1.1	IE 4+ only
queryCommand Indeterm()	Determines whether a specific command is in the indeterminate state	JavaScript 1.1	IE 4+ only
queryCommand State()	Determines the state of a command issued	JavaScript 1.1	IE 4+ only
queryCommand Supported()	Determines whether a specific command is on or off	JavaScript 1.1	IE 4+ only
queryCommand Text()	Determines the string associated with a command	JavaScript 1.1	IE 4+ only
queryCommand Value()	Determines the value argument	JavaScript 1.1	IE 4+ only
write()	Appends data to a document	JavaScript 1.0	
writeln()	Appends data to a new line in a document	JavaScript 1.0	

Table 5-9.   Document Functions and Descriptions *(continued)*

document.activeElement

The activeElement property returns the currently active element (the element that has the focus) in the document.

document.all

The all property is an array of all the elements contained in a document.

document.alinkColor, document.bgColor, document.fgColor, document.linkColor, and document.vlinkColor

The alinkColor, bgColor, fgColor, linkColor, and vlinkColor properties return the color of their <BODY> counterparts, as shown in the following table. Netscape 4 and IE 4+ always return a hexadecimal value, while Netscape 6+ returns the entered value.

Property	Counterpart
alinkColor	ALINK
bgColor	BACKGROUND
fgColor	TEXT
linkColor	LINK
vlinkColor	VLINK

Here's an example, to test the various browser's outputs.

```
<html><head><title>Color Test</title></head>
<body link="blue" text="white" alink="pink"
     vlink="green" bgcolor="black">
<pre>
<script type="text/javascript">
document.write("alinkColor : " + document.alinkColor + "\n");
document.write("bgColor    : " + document.bgColor + "\n");
document.write("fgColor    : " + document.fgColor + "\n");
document.write("linkColor  : " + document.linkColor + "\n");
document.write("vlinkColor : " + document.linkColor + "\n");
</script>
</pre></body></html>
```

document.anchors[]

The anchors[] array contains all the anchors in the page Anchors are represented as <a name="*name*"></a>. This property may also be used with the length property, as documents.anchors.length.

```
var test= document.anchors;
document.write(test);
```

Please note that Netscape 4.x, Netscape 6.x and IE 4+ each return different results for this simple script.

Browser	Returns
Netscape 4+	[object AnchorArray]
Netscape 6+	[object HTMLCollection]
IE 4+	[object AnchorArray]

document.applets[]

The applets[] array contains all the applet objects in the document. This property may also be used with the length property as document.applets.length. You may also request an applet by name as document.applets["*name*"].

document.attributes

The attributes property is an unordered set of attribute information items, one for each of the attributes (specified or defaulted from the DTD) of this element.

document.body

The body property contains the content of the <BODY> element. This property is only available for Netscape 6+ and IE 4+.

document.characterSet

The `characterSet` property contains character set information from the browser. This property is only available for Netscape 6+.

```
var chrset = document.characterSet;
document.write(chrset);
// this returns ISO-8859-1 in my browser.
```

document.childNodes

The `childNodes` property contains information about each element in the document. For example,

```
<html>
<head>
<title>This is the document's title</title>
</head>
<body>
<h3>This is a heading 3</h3>
<p>This is a paragraph.</p>
<p>It contains <BR> several paragraphs.</p>
<p>This paragraph, has several, children.</p>
</body>
</html>
```

This example has two children, HEAD and BODY. The HEAD has a child, TITLE, while the BODY has four children: one H3 and three Ps. The first two Ps have one child, the text contained inside of them. The last P has three children, each set of text delimited by commas.

This changes the text of the last paragraph to new text:

```
document.childNodes[1].childNodes[3].
firstChild.nodeValue = 'new text'
```

document.clear()

The `clear()` method clears the current document. It has been deprecated.

document.close()

The `close()` method displays any output to document that has been written but not displayed; then it closes the output stream to document. When generating HTML pages with `document.write()`, you should invoke `document.close()` when you reach the end of the page.

document.cookie

The `cookie` property returns a boolean value if a cookie is accessed or created by the current document. It either returns `true` or nothing.

document.createElement()

The `createElement()` method dynamically creates `<IMG>` or `<OPTION>` elements and adds them to the Images and Options collections.

```
myOption = documents.createElement("OPTION")
document.forms(index).elements
("<select>Option 1").options.add myOption, 0;
```

document.createStyleSheet()

The `createStyleSheet()` method can be used to create and add a StyleSheet object to the referenced document.

document.defaultCharset

The `defaultCharset` property contains information about the document's default character set. This property only works in IE 4+.

```
var chrset = document.defaultCharset
document.write(document.defaultCharset);
//My computer returns: windows-1252
```

document.documentElement

The `documentElement` property contains root document information about child nodes. This property works in IE 4+ and Netscape 6+.

`document.domain`

The `domain` property can be used to set or return the
security domain for a document, which will allow documents
originating from different servers to communicate with
each other. For example, if you have different servers for
www.webbedtogether.com and test.webbedtogether.com,
documents loaded from each server (perhaps into a framed setup)
would not initially be able to communicate and share properties,
and so on, unless the `document.domain=webbedtogether.com`
property has been set in all the documents that require sharing.

`document.elementFromPoint()`

The `elementFromPoint()` method determines the HTML element
at a given point. The syntax is

`document.elementFromPoint(x,y)`

`document.embeds[]`

The `embeds[]` array contains each embedded object contained in
the document. You may either refer to the number of embedded
element using `document.embeds[0]` or by the name of the element
using `document.embeds["name"]`.This property may also be used
with the `length` property, as follows: `document.embeds.length`.

`document.execCommand()`

The `execCommand()` method can be used to execute a number of
commands over an entire document, or a text range. The syntax is

`object.execCommand(command, boolean, value)`

The options are explained below; Table 5-10 summarizes the
commands that you can use.

`document.expando`

The `expando` property accepts a boolean value, which determines
whether arbitrary properties can be declared for any element in the
document. This property is only available in IE 4+.

Script Section	Description	Required?
command	Command identifier	Yes
boolean	True or false setting indicating whether to show any possible interface that the particular command may have	No
value	A possible value, the contents/ data type of which are determined by the specific command used	No

***Here are the commands that may be used by value in execCommand().

5

Command	Description	Value
BackColor	Sets the background color of the referenced text	#rrggbb | color name
Bold	Wraps a `<B>` element around the referenced object	
Copy	Copies the referenced object to the clipboard	
CreateBookmark	Wraps a `<a name="...">` element around the referenced object	String - bookmark to use
Create Link	Wraps a `<a href="...">` element around the referenced object	String - URL for link
Cut	Copies the referenced object to the clipboard, and then removes it from the document	
Delete	Deletes the referenced object	
FontName	Sets the typeface for the referenced object	String - font name
FontSize	Sets the font size for the referenced object	String - size
ForeColor	Sets the foreground (text) color for the referenced object	#rrggbb | color name
FormatBlock	Wraps a specified block-level element around the referenced object	String - block level element to use
Indent	Indents the referenced object	
InsertButton	Inserts a `<BUTTON>` element at the current insertion point	String - ID value
InsertFieldSet	Inserts a `<FIELDSET>` element at the current insertion point	String - ID value
Insert HorizontalRule	Inserts an `<HR>` element at the current insertion point	String - ID value

Table 5-10.   execCommand() Commands

Command	Description	Value
InsertIFrame	Inserts an `<IFRAME>` element at the current insertion point	String - SRC value
InsertInputButton	Inserts an `<input type="button">` element at the current insertion point	String - ID value
InsertInput Checkbox	Inserts an `<input type="checkbox">` element at the current insertion point	String - ID value
InsertInputFile Upload	Inserts an `<input type= "FileUpload">` element at the current insertion point	String - ID value
InsertInputHidden	Inserts an `<input type="hidden">` element at the current insertion point	String - ID value
InsertInput Password	Inserts an `<input type="password">` element at the current insertion point	String - ID value
InsertInputRadio	Inserts an `<input type="radio">` element at the current insertion point	String - ID value
InsertInputReset	Inserts an `<input type="reset">` element at the current insertion point	String - ID value
InsertInputSubmit	Inserts an `<input type="submit">` element at the current insertion point	String - ID value
InsertInputText	Inserts an `<input type="text">` element at the current insertion point	String - ID value
InsertMarquee	Inserts a `<MARQUEE>` element at the current insertion point	String - ID value
InsertOrderedList	Inserts an `<OL>` element at the current insertion point	String - ID value
InsertParagraph	Inserts a `<P>` element at the current insertion point	String - ID value
InsertSelect Dropdown	Inserts a `<select type="dropdown">` element at the current insertion point	String - ID value
InsertSelect Listbox	Inserts a `<select type="Listbox">` element at the current insertion point	String - ID value
InsertTextArea	Inserts a `<TEXTAREA>` element at the current insertion point	String - ID value
Insert UnorderedList	Inserts a `<UL>` element at the current insertion point	String - ID value
Italic	Wraps an `<I>` element around the referenced object	
JustifyCenter	Centers the referenced object	
JustifyFull	Full justifies the referenced object	
JustifyLeft	Left justifies the referenced object	

Table 5-10.   `execCommand()` Commands *(continued)*

Command	Description	Value
JustifyRight	Right justifies the referenced object	
Outdent	Outdents the referenced object	
OverWrite	Sets the typing mode to insert or overwrite	Boolean - true = overwrite, false = insert
Paste	Places clipboard contents at the current insertion point (can only paste text copied by the copy command in script)	
PlayImage	Starts playing any dynamic images (video, animated GIFs, and so on) with the referenced object	
Refresh	Reloads the source of the current document	
RemoveFormat	Removes formatting for the referenced object	
RemoveParaFormat	Removes any paragraph formatting for the referenced object	
SelectAll	Selects the whole document text	
StopImage	Stops the playing of all dynamic images	
Underline	Wraps a <U> around the referenced object	
Unlink	Removes a link	
Unselect	Empties any selections from the document	

Table 5-10. execCommand() Commands *(continued)*

document.fileCreatedDate

The fileCreatedDate property contains a date when the current document was created. The string returned is in MM/DD/YYYY format. This property is only available in IE 4+.

document.fileModifiedDate

The fileModifiedDate property contains a date when the current document was modified. The string returned is in MM/DD/YYYY format. This property is only available in IE 4+.

document.fileSize

The fileSize property contains the current document's file size. The string returned is the size of the file in bytes. This property is only available in IE 4+.

document.fileUpdatedDate

The fileUpdatedDate property contains the current document's updated date. The string returned is in MM/DD/YYYY format. This property is only available in IE 4+.

document.form

The form object provides access to the attributes of an HTML <FORM> tag and elements within a <FORM> tag as JavaScript properties. It also contains two methods that allow coders to submit and reset forms with JavaScript.

Table 5-11 summarizes the Form object's properties and methods.

Property/Method	Description	JavaScript Version	Notes
acceptCharset	Contains the acceptable character sets	JavaScript 1.4 and higher	Only works in Internet Explorer 5 and higher and Netscape 6
action	The path set in a <FORM> tag's action attribute	JavaScript 1.0 and higher	
elements[]	An array containing references to objects in a form	JavaScript 1.0 and higher	length property only available in JavaScript 1.1 and higher
elements. length	The number of elements in a form	JavaScript 1.1 and higher	Read-only

Table 5-11.   Form Properties and Methods

Property/Method	Description	JavaScript Version	Notes
encoding	The enctype attribute of a form	JavaScript 1.0 and higher	
length	The number of elements in a form		Read-only
method	The HTTP method as set in a <FORM> tag's method attribute	JavaScript 1.0 and higher	
name	The name of a form, as set in a <FORM> tag's name attribute	JavaScript 1.0 and higher	
reset()	Resets a form to its default state	JavaScript 1.0 and higher	
submit()	Submits a form	JavaScript 1.0 and higher	
target	The window or frame target of a form, as set in the <FORM> tag's target attribute	JavaScript 1.0 and higher	

Table 5-11.   Form Properties and Methods *(continued)*

Defining Form Objects

Form objects are created by inserting a <FORM> tag into an HTML page. <FORM> tags have many attributes. In the following HTML code, you can see a <FORM> tag with the attributes that are most often used with JavaScript.

```
<form
  name="myForm"
<!-- name of form (no spaces or dashes) -->
  action="script.cgi"
<!-- path to the file the form submits to -->
  target="parent"
<!-- window or frame to display results in -->
  method="POST"
```

```
<!-- the HTTP method to be used (GET or POST) -->
   enctype="encoding"
<!-- how data will be encoded when submitted -->
   onreset="goReset()"
<!-- function to execute when form is reset -->
   onsubmit="goSubmit()"
<!-- function to execute when form is submitted -->
>
<!-- form elements go here -->
</form>
```

Event handlers used with the Form object are summarized in Table 5-12. Table 5-13 summarizes the objects within the Form object, and the following sections discuss them in detail.

Name	Description	JavaScript Version	Notes
onclick	User clicks one time.	JavaScript 1.0	
ondblclick	User clicks two times.	JavaScript 1.2	Does not work in Navigator 4 on Unix or Mac.
onkeydown	User pushes a key down.	JavaScript 1.2	
onkeypress	User presses a key.	JavaScript 1.2	
onkeyup	User releases a key.	JavaScript 1.2	
onmousedown	User pushes the mouse button down.	JavaScript 1.2	
onmousemove	User moves the mouse.	JavaScript 1.2	
onmouseout	User moves the mouse off of an element.	JavaScript 1.0	
onmouseover	User moves the mouse over an element.	JavaScript 1.0	
onmouseup	User releases the mouse button.	JavaScript 1.2	
onreset	A form reset request.	JavaScript 1.1	
onsubmit	A form submit request.	JavaScript 1.1	

Table 5-12. Event Handlers That Can Be Used with the Form Object

Name	Description	JavaScript Version	Notes
Button	Provides access to button elements in an HTML form	JavaScript 1.0	No constructor; created with HTML
Checkbox	Provides access to checkbox elements in an HTML form	JavaScript 1.0, enhanced in JavaScript 1.1	No constructor; created with HTML
FileUpload	Provides access to file elements in an HTML form	JavaScript 1.0, enhanced in JavaScript 1.1	No constructor; value property not available until JavaScript 1.1
Hidden	Provides access to hidden form elements of an HTML form	JavaScript 1.0	No constructor; created with HTML
Input	Provides access to input elements of an HTML form	JavaScript 1.0, enhanced in JavaScript 1.1	No constructor; created with HTML
Password	Provides access to password fields of an HTML form		No constructor; created with HTML
Select	Provides access to select elements of an HTML form		No constructor; created with HTML
Option	Provides access to option elements of select menus in an HTML form		Constructor available, can also be created with HTML
Radio	Provides access to radio elements in an HTML form		No constructor; created with HTML
Reset	Provides access to reset elements in an HTML form		No constructor; created with HTML
Text	Provides access to text input elements in an HTML form		No constructor; created with HTML
Textarea	Provides access to text area elements of an HTML form		No constructor; created with HTML

Table 5-13.   Objects Within the Form Object

Button

Buttons are the generic push buttons that appear on web pages and don't do anything by default. Don't confuse these generic buttons with submit and reset buttons, which are discussed later in the chapter. Button objects are used to access the button elements in your HTML page through JavaScript.

A Button object is defined by inserting an `<INPUT>` tag with its `type` attribute set to `button` into your HTML form.

```
<form name="myForm">
  <input type="button" name="myButton"
value="Click Me" onClick="clicked()">
</form>
```

Button objects can't be accessed before the button is on the page, so always access a Button object either in a function that will be executed after the page is loaded or in `<SCRIPT>` tags below the button's `<INPUT>` tag in your HTML.

JavaScript can access several properties of buttons: event properties and `value`.

Button objects are available in JavaScript 1.0 and higher.

Button.event   An event property of a Button is initially set to the same value as an event handler property attribute of the `<INPUT>` tag, such as `onclick`, which defines that button in your HTML. The event handlers that can be defined for the button object are `onblur`, `onclick`, `onfocus`, `onmouseup`, and `onmousedown`.

An event property of a Button object should be equal to a function or equal to `null`, or you can simply not set one. If an event property is set to a function, that function will be executed when the event is performed. If an event property is set to `null` or not set, the button will behave normally and no special code will be executed when an event is performed.

An event property of a Button object can be accessed in your JavaScript like this:

```
alert(document.myForm.myButton.onclick);
    // Access onclick event property
    // Alerts function definition code
    // for user determined onclick function
    // This differs between IE and Netscape
```

You can change an event property with JavaScript in two ways. You can either assign a function literal to the event property, as here,

```
document.myForm.myButton.onclick = function()
  { alert("New Function!"); };
    // Assigns a function literal
    // to the onclick property
```

or you can define a function and then assign it to an event property:

```
function functionChange() { alert("New Function!");
  } // define new function
document.myForm.myButton.onclick = functionChange;
    // Assigns a function to the onclick property
    // Note that no parentheses () are used when
    // referencing the function
```

Different event properties are available to the Button object in different versions of JavaScript, as shown in the following table.

Event Handler for Button Object	JavaScript Version	Bugs
onclick	JavaScript 1.0 and higher	Must return a value in Netscape 4 for Macintosh
onblur	JavaScript 1.0 and higher	Doesn't work with buttons in Netscape 3 or lower for Unix
onfocus	JavaScript 1.0 and higher	Doesn't work with buttons in Netscape 3 or lower for Unix
onmousedown	JavaScript 1.2 and higher	
onmouseup	JavaScript 1.2 and higher	

Button.value   The value property of a Button object is initially set to the same value as the value attribute of the `<INPUT>` tag that defines the button in your HTML. This is the text that appears on a button.

Button.value can be accessed in your JavaScript like this:

```
alert(document.myForm.myButton.value);
    // Alerts the value of the Button
```

You can change the value of a button object to any string in your
JavaScript code.

```
document.myForm.myButton.value = "Don't Click Me!";
```

`Button.value` is available in JavaScript 1.0 and higher.

Checkbox

A checkbox is a form element that toggles between checked and
unchecked. Don't confuse checkboxes with radio buttons, which
are discussed later in the chapter.

Checkbox objects are used to access the checkbox elements in your
HTML page through JavaScript.

A Checkbox object is defined by inserting an `<INPUT>` tag with its
`type` attribute set to `checkbox` into your HTML form. They are often
used in groups. To indicate that they are a group, they should all
have the same name.

```
<form name="myForm">
  Where did you hear about us? <br>
  <input type="checkbox" name="myBox"
   value="TV" onClick="clicked()">
  Television <br>
  <input type="checkbox" name="myBox"
   value="Radio" onClick="clicked()">
  On the Radio <br>
  <input type="checkbox" name="myBox"
   value="Other" checked
     onClick="clicked()"> Other <br>
  <!-- This last box is set to be checked by default. -->
</form>
```

Checkbox objects are referred to in JavaScript as an array of objects,
so that `document.myForm.myBox[0]` refers to the first checkbox
on the page, `document.myform.myBox[1]` refers to the second
checkbox on the page, and so on. As in all arrays, the `length`
property is available in JavaScript 1.1 and higher.

Checkboxes have several properties that can be accessed through
JavaScript: event properties, `checked`, `defaultChecked`, and `value`.

Checkbox objects can't be accessed before the checkbox is on the
page, so always access a Checkbox object in either a function that
will be executed after the page is loaded or in `<SCRIPT>` tags below
the checkbox's `<INPUT>` tag in your HTML.

Checkbox objects are available in JavaScript 1.0 and later, and some features are available in JavaScript 1.1 and later.

Checkbox.checked   The checked property of a Checkbox object is a boolean that can be set to either true or false to check and uncheck a box.

Checkbox.checked can be accessed in your JavaScript code like this:

```
var test = document.myForm.myBox[0].checked;
  // test equals true if the first checkbox
  // is checked, false if not
```

You can change the Checkbox.checked property to check and uncheck a box.

```
document.myForm.myBox[0].checked = true;
  // checks the first checkbox
```

Also, you can process all the checkboxes in a set by using the checkbox array's length property.

```
for(var i = 0; i < document.myForm.myBox.length; i++) {
  document.myForm.myBox[i].checked = true;
}
```

Checkbox.checked is available in JavaScript 1.0 and higher.

Checkbox.defaultChecked   The defaultChecked property of a Checkbox object is a read-only boolean that refers to the initial state of a checkbox. The initial state of the checkbox is specified by setting the checked attribute in the <INPUT> tag of your HTML page. If a checkbox is initially checked, defaultChecked equals true. If a checkbox is initially unchecked, defaultChecked equals false.

```
var test = document.myForm.myBox[0].defaultChecked;
  // test equals false
```

Checkbox.defaultChecked is available in JavaScript 1.0 and higher.

Checkbox.event   An event property of a Checkbox object is initially set to the same value as an event handler attribute of the <INPUT> tag, such as onclick, that defines that checkbox in your HTML. The event handlers that can be defined for a Checkbox object are onblur, onclick, and onfocus.

An event property of a Checkbox object should equal a function or null, or you can simply not set one. If an event property is set to a function, that function will be executed when an event is performed. If an event property is set to null or not set, the checkbox will behave normally and no special code will be executed when the event is performed.

An event property can be accessed in your JavaScript like this:

```
alert(document.myForm.myBox[0].onclick);
   // access onclick event property
   // Alerts function definition code for the onClick
   // function
   // This is different between IE and Netscape
```

You can change an event property with JavaScript in two ways. You can either assign a function literal to the event property, as here,

```
document.myForm.myBox[0].onclick = function()
{ alert("New Function!"); };
   // Assigns a function literal to the onclick property
```

or you can define a function and then assign it to the event property:

```
function functionChange()
{ alert("New Function!"); } // define new function
document.myForm.myBox[0].onclick = functionChange;
   // Assigns a function to the onclick property
   // Note that no parentheses () are used when
   // referencing the function
```

Different event properties are available to the Checkbox object in different versions of JavaScript, as shown here:

Event Handler for Checkbox Object	JavaScript Version	Bugs
onblur	JavaScript 1.0 and higher	Doesn't work with checkboxes in Netscape 3 and lower for Unix
onclick	JavaScript 1.0 and higher	Must return a value in Netscape 4 for Macintosh
onfocus	JavaScript 1.0 and higher	Doesn't work with checkboxes in Netscape 3 and lower for Unix

Checkbox.value   The `value` property of a Checkbox object is initially set to the same value as the `value` attribute of the `<INPUT>` tag that defines the checkbox in your HTML. This is the text that would be submitted if the checkbox were checked. It is not normally displayed on an HTML page.

`Checkbox.value` can be accessed in your JavaScript like this:

```
alert(document.myForm.myBox[0].value);
// Alerts the value of the Checkbox
```

You can change the value of a checkbox to any string in your JavaScript code.

```
document.myForm.myBox[0].value = "Television";
```

`Checkbox.value` is available in JavaScript 1.0 and later.

FileUpload

A file upload is a special form element that lets users browse for a file on their hard drive. It looks just like a one-line text box, except it has a Browse button next to it. After the user clicks Browse and chooses a file, the system-specific path to that file appears in the box.

FileUpload objects are used to access the file upload elements in your HTML page through JavaScript.

A FileUpload object is defined by inserting an `<INPUT>` tag with its `type` attribute set to `file` into your HTML form.

```
<form name="myForm">
  Upload File: <input type="file" name="myFile">
</form>
```

The FileUpload object has several properties that can be accessed through JavaScript: event properties and `value`.

FileUpload objects can't be accessed before the file upload element is on the page, so always access a FileUpload object either in a function that will be executed after the page is loaded or in `<SCRIPT>` tags below the file upload element's `<INPUT>` tag in your HTML.

The FileUpload object is available in JavaScript 1.0 and later.

FileUpload.event   An event property of a FileUpload object is initially set to the same value as the event handler attribute of the `<INPUT>` tag, such as `onchange`, which defines that file upload field in your HTML. The event handlers that can be defined for a FileUpload object are onblur, onchange, and onfocus.

An event property can be accessed in your JavaScript like this:

```
alert(document.myForm.myFile.onchange);
   // Accesses the onchange event property
   // Alerts function definition code for the onChange function
   // This is different between IE and Netscape
```

You can change an event property with JavaScript in two ways. You can either assign a function literal to the event property, as here,

```
document.myForm.myFile.onchange = function()
{ alert("New Function!"); };
   // Assigns a function literal to the onchange event property
```

or you can define a function and then assign it to an event property:

```
function functionChange() { alert("New Function!");
   } // define new function
document.myForm.myFile.onchange = functionChange;
   // Assigns a function to the onchange property
   // Note that no parentheses () are used when referencing
   // the function
```

Different event properties are available to the FileUpload object in different versions of JavaScript, as shown here:

Event Handler for FileUpload Object	JavaScript Version	Bugs
onblur	JavaScript 1.0 and higher	
onchange	JavaScript 1.0 and higher	onchange can't access the value property in Netscape 2.0
onfocus	JavaScript 1.0 and higher	

FileUpload.value   The value object of a FileUpload object is a read-only string equal to the value of the file upload field, which is set by the user.

`FileUpload.value` can be accessed in your JavaScript like this:

```
alert(document.myForm.myFile.value);
   // alerts the value of the file upload field, usually a file path
```

`FileUpload.value` can't be changed in your JavaScript code or set using a `value` attribute in the `<INPUT>` tag that defines your file upload field. This helps prevent security problems that might be caused if coders could pick which file they wanted from a person's computer.

`FileUpload.value` is available in JavaScript 1.1 and higher. It isn't available in Netscape 2.0, but is available in Internet Explorer 3.0.

Hidden

5

A hidden field is a form element that users can't see. Hidden fields can be useful for storing data that will be used by both client-side and server-side scripts before and after a form is submitted.

Hidden objects are used to access the hidden form elements in your HTML page through JavaScript. A Hidden object is defined by inserting an `<INPUT>` tag with its `type` attribute set to `hidden` into your HTML form.

```
<form name="myForm">
  <input type="hidden" name=
  "myHiddenField" value="Special Data">
</form>
```

The Hidden object has one property that can be accessed through JavaScript, which is `value`. Hidden objects can't be accessed before the hidden form element is on the page, so always access a Hidden object in either a function that will be executed after the page is loaded or in `<SCRIPT>` tags below the hidden form element's `<INPUT>` tag in your HTML.

The Hidden object is available in JavaScript 1.0 and later.

Hidden.value   The `value` property of a Hidden object is initially set to the same value as the `value` attribute of the `<INPUT>` tag that defines the hidden field in your HTML. `Hidden.value` can be accessed in your JavaScript like this:

```
alert(document.myForm.myHiddenField.value);
   // Alerts the value of the hidden field
```

You can change the value of a hidden field to any string in your JavaScript code.

```
document.myForm.myHiddenField.value = "Really Special Data";
```

`Hidden.value` is available in JavaScript 1.0 and later.

Input

An input element can be a variety of different kinds of form elements, depending on how the `type` attribute of the `<INPUT>` tag is set in an HTML page.

The Input object provides access to input elements on HTML pages through JavaScript. An Input object can be defined by inserting an `<INPUT>` tag into your HTML form.

```
<form name="myForm">
  <input type="text" name="myInput">
    <!-- This input tag's type attribute
         is set to text,
         but it could have been set
         to one of many things. -->
</form>
```

Input objects can't be accessed before the input element is on the page, so always access an Input object either in a function that will be executed after the page is loaded or in `<SCRIPT>` tags below the `<INPUT>` tag in your HTML.

Input objects are available in JavaScript 1.0 and later, and some features are only available in JavaScript 1.1 and later.

Input.blur()   The `blur()` method of an Input object removes the focus of the page from the input element. The element on the page that is focused is the selected one that can be typed into or clicked with the keyboard.

`Input.blur()` can be executed in your JavaScript like this:

```
document.myForm.myTextBox.blur();
 // un-focuses a text element
```

`Input.blur()` is available in JavaScript 1.0 and later. In Netscape 2 and 3 for Unix, `Input.blur()` only works for text fields, password

fields, text areas, and file upload fields. Also see
"Input.focus()," which has the opposite effect.

Input.checked   The checked property of an Input object is
available in checkboxes and radio buttons. checked is a boolean
that can be tested or set to either true or false to check and
uncheck a checkbox or radio button.

Input.checked can be accessed in your JavaScript code like this:

```
var test = document.myForm.myBox[0].checked;
  // test equals true if the first
  // checkbox is checked, false if not
```

You can change the Checkbox.checked property to check and
uncheck a checkbox or radio button.

```
document.myForm.myBox[0].checked = true;
  // checks the first checkbox in a set
document.myForm.myRadio[0].checked = true;
  // checks the first radio button in a set
```

Input.checked is available in JavaScript 1.0 and higher.

See "Checkbox.checked," earlier, and "Radio.checked," later,
for more information. Also see "Input.click()," which can be
used for the same results.

Input.click()   The click() method of an Input object can
be used to simulate clicking a checkbox, button, submit button, or
reset button.

Input.click can be executed in your JavaScript like this:

```
document.myForm.myButton.click();
  // simulate clicking a button
```

Input.click() can often do the job of form.submit and
form.reset for submit and reset buttons, and can be used instead
of using the checked property with checkboxes and radio buttons.

Input.click() is available in JavaScript 1.0 and later. However,
click() only executes a form element's onclick handler in
Netscape 4 and higher and Internet Explorer 4 and higher.

Input.defaultChecked   The defaultChecked property of
an Input object is a read-only boolean that refers to the initial state

5

of a checkbox or radio button. The initial state of the checkbox or radio button is specified by setting the `checked` attribute in the `<INPUT>` tag in your HTML page. If a checkbox is initially checked, `defaultChecked` equals `true`. If a checkbox is initially unchecked, `defaultChecked` equals `false`.

```
var test = document.myForm.myBox[0].defaultChecked;
 // test equals false
```

`Input.defaultChecked` is available in JavaScript 1.0 and higher.

Input.defaultValue   The `defaultValue` property of a form element returns the initial value of a text box, text area, or password field. The initial value is defined in the `value` attribute of an `<INPUT>` tag.

`Input.defaultValue` can be accessed in your code like this:

```
alert(document.myForm.myTextBox.defaultValue);
 // alerts the default value of a text input element
```

`Input.defaultValue` is available in JavaScript 1.0 and later.

Input.focus()   The `focus()` method of an Input object sends the focus of the page to that object. The element on the page that is focused is the selected one that can be typed into or clicked with the keyboard.

`Input.focus()` can be executed in your JavaScript like this:

```
document.myForm.myTextBox.focus(); // focuses a text element
```

`Input.focus()` is available in JavaScript 1.0 and later. In Netscape 2 and 3 for Unix, `Input.focus()` only works for text fields, password fields, text areas, and file upload fields.

Also see "`Input.blur()`," which has the opposite effect.

Input.form   The `form` attribute of an Input object is a read-only property that contains a reference to the Form object where the Input object is contained. `Input.form` is most often used with `this` in an event handler attribute in HTML `<INPUT>` tags. For example, you can use a button to change the action of your form like this:

```
<form name="myForm" action="script.cgi" method="POST">
  <input type="button" name=
"myButton" value="Change Form Action"
    onclick="this.form.action='new_script.cgi'">
</form>
  // <!Clicking the "Change Form Action"
     button changes the form's action
  // to new_script.cgi -->
```

Input.form is available in JavaScript 1.0 and higher.

Input.length   This property is available in Select objects only. See "Select.length" later in the chapter.

Input.name   The name property of an Input object is initially equal to the name attribute of the <INPUT> tag in your HTML. This is the name you use in JavaScript when you refer to the Input object that correlates to an input element. This is also the name that will be associated with the Input object's value when the form's data is passed to a script.

You can access the name property in your code like this:

```
alert(document.myForm.myTextBox.name);
  // alerts the name of a textbox
```

Or you can change the name of an Input object. In this example, we'll change the name of a button:

```
document.myForm.myTextBox.name = 'myTextBox2';
  // Changes the name of myTextBox to myTextBox2.
  // In later code, we'll have to
  // refer to myTextBox as myTextBox2.
```

Input.name is available in JavaScript 1.0 and later.

Also see "Input.value."

Input.options[]   This array is available in Select objects only. See "Select.options[]," later in the chapter.

Input.select()   The Input.select() method selects all the text in a text field, text area, password field, or file upload field. When the text in a field is selected, in most browsers it can be cut, pasted, deleted, or automatically deleted or typed over.

A bug prevents the text of an element from being selected in Netscape if it doesn't have the input focus of the page, so you should always use the `focus()` method before you use the `select()` method. We'll use that workaround in the following example.

```
document.myForm.myTextBox.focus();
 // focus a form element first
document.myForm.myTextBox.select();
 // select the text in the form element
```

`Input.select()` is available in JavaScript 1.0 and later, but doesn't work in Netscape 2.0.

Input.selectedIndex   This property is available in Select objects only. See "`Select.selectedIndex`," later in the chapter.

Input.type   The `Input.type` property of an Input object specifies the type of a given Input object. This is useful when you need to test whether an element is a checkbox or a radio button, for example. `Input.type` is a read-only string.

See Table 5-14 for the specific string returned by the `type` property of each kind of Input object.

Input Object	`type` String	HTML Tag for Input Object
Button	button	`<input type="button">`
Checkbox	checkbox	`<input type="checkbox">`
FileUpload	file	`<input type="file">`
Hidden	hidden	`<input type="hidden">`
Password	password	`<input type="password">`
Radio	radio	`<input type="radio">`
Reset	reset	`<input type="reset">`
Select (without multiple)	select-one	`<select></select>`
Select (with multiple)	select-multiple	`<select multiple></select>`
Submit	submit	`<input type="submit">`
Text	text	`<input type="text">`
Textarea	textarea	`<textarea></textarea>`

Table 5-14.   Strings Contained in `Input.type` for Different Input Objects

`Input.type` is available in JavaScript 1.1 and later.

Input.value   The `value` property of an Input object is initially equal to the `value` attribute of the `<INPUT>` tag in your HTML. This is the value that is passed to the script that a form submits to when the form is submitted.

You can access `Input.value` in your code like this:

```
alert(document.myForm.myTextBox.value);
  // alerts the value of a textbox
```

`Input.value` can also be modified by your scripts. You can change the `value` of an Input object like this:

```
document.myForm.myTextBox.value = "New Textbox Value";
  // changes the value of a textbox to
    "New Textbox Value".
```

Most Input elements display their value in the browser window, so modifying the value of an input element with JavaScript can give your form a dynamic look. The following table summarizes how each Input object's value is normally displayed in a browser.

Input Object Type	`value` Is Displayed As
Button, Reset, Submit	The text on the button
Text, Textarea, FileUpload	The text inside the text box
Password	Asterisks in the same quantity of characters in the `value`, displayed inside the text box
Checkbox, Radio, Hidden	`value` is not displayed
Select	`value` is not used

`Input.value` is available in Netscape 2 and higher, and Internet Explorer 3 and higher.

Option
Options are the menu items that appear in select menus. The Option object provides access to input elements on HTML pages through JavaScript.

Option objects are normally specified with <OPTION> tags, which must be between <SELECT> tags. You can create new Option objects in your HTML like this:

```
<form name="myForm">
  <select name="mySelect">
    <option value="Yahoo">Yahoo!</option>
    <option selected>Google</option>
    <option>dmoz.org</option>
  </select>
</form>
```

When you write <OPTION> tags, you can give them an optional value attribute. If you don't set a value attribute, the value of the option will be the text between the <OPTION> tags.

You can also give your <OPTION> tags an optional selected attribute that will make them selected by default.

The Option() Constructor   New Option objects can also be created using a constructor. These dynamically add new options to the menus on your page.

The Option() constructor takes four arguments. The first argument is the text of the option, the second is the optional value, the third is whether the option is selected by default or not, and the fourth is whether the option is selected or not. The third and fourth arguments should be either 1, for selected, or 0, for not selected.

In the following example, we'll add a new option to our menu.

```
document.myForm.mySelect.options[3] =
    new Option("GoTo.com","goto");
  // adds a 4th option to the search menu
```

The Option() constructor is available in JavaScript 1.1 and higher.

Option.defaultSelected   The defaultSelected property of an Option object is a read-only boolean value that is true if the option is selected by default, false if not. This value is initially set to true by setting the selected attribute of the <OPTION> tag in your HTML.

You can access Option.defaultSelected in your code like this:

```
var test = document.myForm.mySelect.options[1].defaultSelected;
  // test equals true when the 2nd option is selected by default
```

`Option.defaultSelected` is available in JavaScript 1.0 and later.

Option.index   The `index` property of an Option object is equal to the index of an option in a Select object's `options[]` array. Options are initially ordered from the first to appear in your HTML code to the last, starting from zero for the first element. `Options.index` is read-only.

`Options.index` can be accessed in your JavaScript like this:

```
var i = document.myForm.mySelect.options[2].index;
    // i equals 2. Isn't this redundant?
```

`Options.index` is available in JavaScript 1.0 and higher.

Option.selected   The `selected` property of an Option object is a boolean value that is `true` if the option is selected, `false` if not. This value is initially set to `true` by setting the `selected` attribute of the `<OPTION>` tag in your HTML.

You can access `Option.selected` in your code like this:

```
var test =
document.myForm.mySelect.options[1].selected;
    // test equals true if the 2nd option is selected
```

You can also change the value of `Option.selected` in your code to select and deselect an option.

```
document.myForm.mySelect.options[1].selected=false;
    // the 2nd options of search is no longer selected
```

`Option.selected` is available in JavaScript 1.0 and later.

Option.text   The `text` property of an Option object is equal to the text that is displayed on the option in a select menu on the page. The initial value of `Option.text` is the text between the opening and closing `<OPTION>` tags that defines an option in your HTML.

`Option.text` is the value that is sent to a script when the form is submitted if no `value` is defined for that option. You can access `Option.text` in your JavaScript code like this:

```
alert(document.myForm.mySelect.options[2]text);
    // alerts the text of an option, "dmoz.org"
```

You can also change the value of `Option.text` in JavaScript 1.1 and later. This changes the text that is displayed for an option in the browser.

```
document.myForm.mySelect.options[2].text =
 "Open Directory Project";
  // changes the text of an option
```

`Option.text` is read-only in JavaScript 1.0 and later, and is readable and writable in JavaScript 1.1 and later.

Option.value   The `value` property of an Option object is an optional value to be submitted to a script when the form is submitted. This is initially set by defining a `value` attribute in the `<OPTION>` tag in your HTML.

You can access `Option.value` in your JavaScript code like this:

```
var v = document.myForm.mySelect.options[1].value;
 // v equals "Yahoo"
```

`Option.value` can be changed to any string, like this:

```
document.myForm.mySelect.options[1].value = "Yahoo Directory";
```

`Option.value` is available in JavaScript 1.0 and later.

Password

Password fields are text fields that conceal what the user types. In most browsers, they display asterisks for each character typed. The initial value of a password field can be set in the `value` property of the `<INPUT>` tag that defines your password field.

Password objects are used to access the password fields in your HTML page through JavaScript.

A Password object is defined by inserting an `<INPUT>` tag with its `type` attribute set to `password` into your HTML form.

```
<form name="myForm">
   <input type="password" name=
   "myPassword" value="pAss" onclick="clicked()">
</form>
```

Password objects can't be accessed before the password field is on the page, so always access a Password object either in a function that will be executed after the page is loaded or in <SCRIPT> tags below the password field's <INPUT> tag in your HTML.

JavaScript can access several properties of password fields: event properties and value.

Password objects are available in JavaScript 1.0 and higher.

Password.event   An event property of a Password is initially set to the same value as an event handler property attribute of the <INPUT> tag that defines that password field in your HTML, such as onchange. The event handlers that can be defined for the password field are onblur, onchange, and onfocus.

An event property of a Password object should be equal to a function or equal to null, or you can simply not set one. If an event property is set to a function, that function will be executed when the event is performed. If an event property is set to null or not set, the form field will behave normally and no special code will be executed when an event is performed.

An event property of a Password object can be accessed in your JavaScript like this:

```
alert(document.myForm.myPassword.onchange);
 // Access onclick event property
  // Alerts function definition code
  // for user determined onchange function
  // This differs between IE and Netscape
```

You can change an event property with JavaScript in two ways. You can either assign a function literal to the event property, as here,

```
document.myForm.myPassword.onchange = function()
 { alert("New Function"); };
  // Assigns a function literal to the onclick property
```

or you can define a function and then assign it to an event property:

```
function functionChange() { alert("New Function!");
 } // define new function
document.myForm.myPassword.onchange=functionChange;
```

```
// Assigns a function to the onchange property
// Note that no parentheses () are used
// when referencing the function
```

Different event properties are available to the Password object in different versions of JavaScript, as shown in the following table.

Event Handler for Password Object	JavaScript Version	Bugs
onBlur()	JavaScript 1.0 and higher	
onChange()	JavaScript 1.0 and higher	
onFocus()	JavaScript 1.0 and higher	

Password.value   The value property of a Radio object is initially set to the same value as the value attribute of the <INPUT> tag that defines the password field in your HTML. This is the text that will be submitted to a script if a form is submitted. The value is not displayed on an HTML page, but most browsers display an asterisk for each character.

Password.value can't be accessed in JavaScript 1.0 and 1.1 after it has been changed from its initial value. In JavaScript 1.2 and higher, you can read the new value. You can access this value like this:

```
alert(document.myForm.myPassword.value);
// Alerts the value of the password
```

Password.value is read-only in practice, not in theory. Although you can change the value of the Password object in your code, when the form is submitted, the browser will submit either the value the user last entered or the initial value of the field that was specified in its value attribute.

Password.value is available in JavaScript 1.0 and later.

Radio

A radio button is a form element that represents a group of mutually exclusive options. You might use radio buttons, for example, in an order form in which you ask a customer how she would like her order shipped—by UPS, FedEx, or DHL. In this example, the customer can choose no more than one option. Don't confuse radio buttons with checkboxes, which were discussed earlier.

Radio objects are used to access the radio button elements in your HTML page through JavaScript. A Radio object is defined by inserting an <INPUT> tag with its type attribute set to radio into your HTML form. They are almost always used in groups. To indicate that they are a group, they should all have the same name.

```
<form name="myForm">
  How would you like your order shipped? <br>
  <input type="radio" name="myRadio"
   value="ups" onClick="clicked()">
  UPS <br>
  <input type="radio" name="myRadio"
   value="fedex" onClick="clicked()">
  FedEx <br>
  <input type="radio" name="myRadio"
   value="dhl" checked
    onClick="clicked()"> DHL
  <!-- This last box is set to
  be checked by default. -->
</form>
```

Radio objects are referred to in JavaScript as an array of objects, so that document.myForm.myRadio[0] refers to the first radio button on the page, document.myform.myRadio[1] refers to the second radio button on the page, and so on. As in all arrays, the length property is available in JavaScript 1.1 and higher.

Radio buttons have several properties that can be accessed through JavaScript: event properties, checked, defaultChecked, and value.

Radio objects can't be accessed before the radio button is on the page, so always access a Radio object either in a function that will be executed after the page is loaded or in <SCRIPT> tags below the radio button's <INPUT> tag in your HTML.

Radio objects are available in JavaScript 1.0 and later, and some features are available in JavaScript 1.1 and later.

Radio.checked   The `checked` property of a Radio object is a boolean that can be set to either `true` or `false` to check and uncheck a radio button.

`Radio.checked` can be accessed in your JavaScript code like this:

```
var test = document.myForm.myRadio[0].checked;
  // test equals true if the first
  // button is checked, false if not
```

You can change the `Radio.checked` property to check and uncheck a button.

```
document.myForm.myRadio[0].checked = true;
  // checks the first button
```

Also, you can process all the checkboxes in a set by using the radio box array's `length` property.

```
for(var i = 0; i < document.myForm.myRadio.length;
  i++) {
   if (document.myForm.myRadio.checked)
{ oneIsChecked.checked = true; }
}
```

`Radio.checked` is available in JavaScript 1.0 and higher.

Radio.defaultChecked   The `defaultChecked` property of a Radio object is a read-only boolean that refers to the initial state of a radio button. The initial state of a radio button is specified by setting the `checked` attribute in the `<INPUT>` tag of your HTML page. If a radio button is initially checked, `defaultChecked` equals `true`. If a radio button is initially unchecked, `defaultChecked` equals `false`.

```
var test = document.myForm.myRadio[0].defaultChecked;
  // test equals false
```

`Radio.defaultChecked` is available in JavaScript 1.0 and higher.

Radio.event   An event property of a Radio object is initially set to the same value as an event handler attribute of the `<INPUT>` tag that defines that radio button in your HTML, such as `onclick`. The event handlers that can be defined for a Radio object are `onblur`, `onclick`, and `onfocus`.

An event property of a Radio object should equal a function or
`null`, or you can simply not set one. If an event property is set
to a function, that function will be executed when an event is
performed. If an event property is set to `null` or not set, the
radio button will behave normally and no special code will be
executed when the event is performed.

An event property can be accessed in your JavaScript like this:

```
alert(document.myForm.myRadio[0].onclick);
 // access onclick event property
  // Alerts function definition code for the onClick function
  // This is different between IE and Netscape
```

You can change an event property with JavaScript in two ways.
You can either assign a function literal to the event property,
as here,

```
document.myForm.myRadio[0].onclick = function()
 { alert("New Function!"); };
  // Assigns a function literal to the onclick property
```

or you can define a function and then assign it to the event property:

```
function functionChange() { alert("New Function!");
 }
 // define new function
    document.myForm.myRadio[0].onclick = functionChange;
  // Assigns a function to the onclick property
  // Note that no parentheses () are
  // used when referencing the function
```

Different event properties are available to the Radio object in
different versions of JavaScript, as shown in the following table.

Event Handler for Radio Object	JavaScript Version	Bugs
onblur	JavaScript 1.0 and higher	Doesn't work with checkboxes in Netscape 3 and lower for Unix
onclick	JavaScript 1.0 and higher	Must return a value in Netscape 4 for Macintosh
onfocus	JavaScript 1.0 and higher	Doesn't work with checkboxes in Netscape 3 and lower for Unix

5

Radio.value   The `value` property of a Radio object is initially set to the same value as the `value` attribute of the `<INPUT>` tag that defines the radio button in your HTML. This is the text that would be submitted if the radio button were checked. It is not normally displayed on an HTML page.

`Radio.value` can be accessed in your JavaScript like this:

```
alert(document.myForm.myRadio[0].value);
  // Alerts the value of the Button
```

You can change the value of a radio button in your JavaScript code to any string.

```
document.myForm.myRadio[0].value = "fed-ex";
```

`Radio.value` is available in JavaScript 1.0 and later.

Reset

Reset buttons set a form back to its default values. They often are called "clear" buttons. Don't confuse them with generic buttons or submit, which are discussed in their own sections.

Reset objects are used to access the reset button elements in your HTML page through JavaScript. A Reset object is defined by inserting an `<INPUT>` tag with its `type` attribute set to `reset` into your HTML form.

```
<form name="myForm">
  <input type="reset" name="myReset"
   value="Reset Form" onClick="clicked()">
</form>
```

Reset objects can't be accessed before the button is on the page, so always access a Reset object either in a function that will be executed after the page is loaded or in `<SCRIPT>` tags below the reset button's `<INPUT>` tag in your HTML.

JavaScript can access several properties of reset buttons: event properties and `value`.

Reset objects are available in JavaScript 1.0 and higher.

Reset.event   An event property of a Reset object is initially set to the same value as an event handler property attribute of the <INPUT> tag that defines that button in your HTML, such as onclick. The event handlers that can be defined for the reset button object are onblur, onclick, onfocus, onmouseup, and onmousedown.

An event property of a Reset object should be equal to a function or equal to null, or you can simply not set one. If an event property is set to a function, that function will be executed when the event is performed. If an event property is set to null or not set, the button will behave normally and no special code will be executed when an event is performed.

An event property of a Reset object can be accessed in your JavaScript like this:

```
alert(document.myForm.myReset.onclick);
  // Access onclick event property
  // Alerts function definition code
  // for user determined onclick function
  // This differs between IE and Netscape
```

You can change an event property with JavaScript in two ways. You can either assign a function literal to the event property, as here,

```
document.myForm.myReset.onclick = function()
{ alert("New Function!"); };
  // Assigns a function literal to the
  // onclick property
```

or you can define a function and then assign it to an event property:

```
function functionChange() { alert("New Function!");
}
// define new function
document.myForm.myReset.onclick = functionChange;
  // Assigns a function to the onclick property
  // Note that no parentheses () are used
  // when referencing the function
```

Different event properties are available to the Reset object in different versions of JavaScript, as shown in the following table.

Event Handler for Reset Object	JavaScript Version	Bugs
onclick	JavaScript 1.0 and higher	Must return a value to work in Netscape 4 for Macintosh
onblur	JavaScript 1.0 and higher	Doesn't work with buttons in Netscape 3 and lower for Unix
onfocus	JavaScript 1.0 and higher	Doesn't work with buttons in Netscape 3 and lower for Unix
onmousedown	JavaScript 1.2 and higher	
onmouseup	JavaScript 1.2 and higher	

Reset.value   The value property of a Reset object is initially set to the same value as the value attribute of the <INPUT> tag that defines the reset button in your HTML. This is the text that appears on the reset button.

Reset.value can be accessed in your JavaScript like this:

```
alert(document.myForm.myReset.value);
  // Alerts the value of the Reset
```

You can also change the value of a Reset object to any string in your JavaScript code. This changes the appearance of the button on the page.

```
document.myForm.myReset.value = "Don't Click Me!";
```

Reset.value is available in JavaScript 1.0 and higher.

Select

Select menus are the lists of options that are sometimes called drop-down menus. They allow a user to select one option from a list or multiple options, depending on how the menu is defined in your HTML. The Select object provides access to the select menu elements on HTML pages through JavaScript.

You can create a select menu by placing a <SELECT> tag in your HTML. The tag should always contain at least one <OPTION> tag, and should always have a closing </SELECT> tag at the end. Optionally, the <SELECT> tag can contain a size attribute that equals the height of the menu (in options) or the multiple attribute, which allows users to select more than one item in the menu.

```
<form name="myForm" size="3" multiple>
  <select name="mySelect" size="">
    <option value="Yahoo">Yahoo!</option>
    <option selected>Google</option>
    <option>dmoz.org</option>
  </select>
</form>
```

Select objects can't be accessed before the select menu is on the page, so always access a Select object either in a function that will be executed after the page is loaded or in <SCRIPT> tags below the <SELECT> tag in your HTML.

JavaScript can access several properties of select menus: event properties, length, options, selectedIndex, and value.

Select objects are available in JavaScript 1.0 and higher, and some features are available in JavaScript 1.1 and higher.

Select.event   An event property of a Select is initially set to the same value as an event handler property attribute of the <INPUT> tag that defines that select menu in your HTML, such as onchange. The event handlers that can be defined for the password field are onblur, onchange, and onfocus.

An event property of a Select object should be equal to a function or equal to null, or you can simply not set one. If an event property is set to a function, that function will be executed when the event is performed. If an event property is set to null or not set, the select menu will behave normally and no special code will be executed when an event is performed.

An event property of a Select object can be accessed in your JavaScript like this:

```
alert(document.myForm.mySelect.onchange);
  // Access onchange event property
  // Alerts function definition code
  // for user determined onchange function
  // This differs between IE and Netscape
```

You can change an event property with JavaScript in two ways. You can either assign a function literal to the event property, as here,

```
document.myForm.mySelect.onchange = function()

{ alert("New Function!"); };

  // Assigns a function literal to
     the onclick property
```

or you can define a function and then assign it to an event property:

```
function functionChange() { alert("New Function!");
} // define new function
      document.myForm.mySelect.onchange = functionChange;
  // Assigns a function to the onchange property
  // Note that no parentheses () are used when
  // referencing the function
```

Different event properties are available to the Select object in different versions of JavaScript, as shown in this table:

Event Handler for Select Object	JavaScript Version	Bugs
onBlur()	JavaScript 1.0 and higher	Doesn't work with select menus in Netscape 3 and lower for Unix.
onChange()	JavaScript 1.0 and higher	In Netscape 2, the onchange event is not invoked until the menu loses input focus.
onFocus()	JavaScript 1.0 and higher	Doesn't work with select menus in Netscape 3 and lower for Unix.

Select.length   The Select.length property is equal to the number of options in a select menu. It is read-only. Select.length can be accessed in your JavaScript code like this:

```
alert("My menu has " + document.myForm.mySelect.length + " options.");
// alerts the number of options in a select menu
```

`Select.length` is available in JavaScript 1.0 and later.

Select.options[]   The `Select.options[]` array contains references to the Option objects that represent the options of a select menu. These are initially listed in the order in which they appear in your HTML.

You can access `Select.options[]` in your JavaScript code like this:

```
alert("My menu has these options: " + document.myForm.mySelect.options[] );
// alerts a list of the options in a form
```

You can use `options[]` to process all the options in your select menu in a loop.

```
for(var i=0; i < document.myForm.mySelect.options.length; i++) {
            document.myForm.mySelect.options[i].value = "";
}
// clears the value of each of
   the options in a select menu
```

In JavaScript 1.1 and higher, `Select.options[]` can also be modified. You can set the length to a lower number to truncate extra options from the end of your menu, like this:

```
document.myForm.mySelect.options.length = 1;
  // deletes all but the first option
  // in a select menu
```

You can also create a new option in a select menu by adding it to the `options[]` array:

```
document.myForm.mySelect.options[3] = new Option("GoTo.com","goto");
  // adds a 4th option to a select menu
```

Options in an array can be deleted by setting the value of an object in the `Select.options[]` array to `null`. When this is done, the indexes of the other elements in the `options[]` array are shifted automatically to fill in the "empty space."

```
document.myForm.mySelect.options[3] = null;
   // deletes the 4th option from a select menu
```

`Select.options[]` is available in JavaScript 1.0 and later, and is read/write in JavaScript 1.1 and later.

Select.selectedIndex   The `selectedIndex` property of a Select object is equal to the index of the option that is selected in a select menu. If there is no option selected, this property is equal to –1.

`Select.selectedIndex` can be accessed in your JavaScript code like this:

```
var i = document.myForm.mySelect.selectedIndex;
   // i equals 2, if the third option was selected.
```

If the `multiple` attribute is set in your `<SELECT>` tag, you should use a loop instead of `selectedIndex` to determine which items are selected, like this:

```
var selected[] = new Array(); for(var i=0; i
   < document.myForm.mySelect.options.length; i++)
   {if (document.myForm.mySelect.options[i].selected)
   alert(document.myForm.mySelect.options[i] + " is selected.";
   // alerts a message when an option is selected
}
```

In JavaScript 1.1, you can write to the `selectedIndex` property to select any option in a select menu.

```
document.myForm.mySelect.selectedIndex = 0;
   // selects the first option in a select menu
```

The `Select.selectedIndex` property is available in JavaScript 1.0 and is read/write in JavaScript 1.1.

Select.type   The `type` property of a Select object is equal to one of two strings that tell whether the select menu allows multiple selections or not. If the menu allows multiple selections, then `type` is equal to "select-multiple." Otherwise, `type` is equal to "select-one." `Select.type` is read-only.

`Select.type` can be accessed in your JavaScript code like this:

```
alert("My menu is a " + document.myForm.mySelect.type + "menu.");
  // alerts the type of a select menu
```

`Select.type` is available in JavaScript 1.1 and later.

Submit

Submit buttons send a form's data to the script that was specified in a <FORM> tag's `action` attribute. Don't confuse them with generic buttons or reset buttons, which are discussed in their own sections. Submit objects are used to access the submit button elements in your HTML page through JavaScript.

A Submit object is defined by inserting an <INPUT> tag with its `type` attribute set to `submit` into your HTML form.

```
<form name="myForm">
  <input type="submit" name="mySubmit"
  value="Submit" onClick="clicked()">
</form>
```

Submit objects can't be accessed before the button is on the page, so always access a Submit object either in a function that will be executed after the page is loaded or in <SCRIPT> tags below the reset button's <INPUT> tag in your HTML.

JavaScript can access several properties of submit buttons: event properties and `value`.

Submit objects are available in JavaScript 1.0 and higher.

Submit.event   An event property of a Submit object is initially set to the same value as an event handler property attribute of the <INPUT> tag that defines the submit button in your HTML, such as `onclick`. The event handlers that can be defined for a submit button object are `onblur`, `onclick`, `onfocus`, `onmouseup`, and `onmousedown`.

An event property of a Submit object should be equal to a function or equal to `null`, or you can simply not set one. If an event property is set to a function, that function will be executed when the event is performed. If an event property is set to `null` or not set, the button will behave normally and no special code will be executed when an event is performed.

An event property of a Submit object can be accessed in your JavaScript like this:

```
alert(document.myForm.mySubmit.onclick);
  // Access onclick event property
   // Alerts function definition code
   // for user determined onclick function
   // This differs between IE and Netscape
```

You can change an event property with JavaScript in two ways. You can either assign a function literal to the event property, as here,

```
document.myForm.mySubmit.onclick =
function() { alert("New Function!"); };
   // Assigns a function literal to
   // the onclick property
```

or you can define a function and then assign it to an event property:

```
function functionChange()
{ alert("New Function!"); } // define new function
document.myForm.mySubmit.onclick = functionChange;
   // Assigns a function to the onclick property
   // Note that no parentheses () are used when
   // referencing the function
```

Different event properties are available to the Submit object in different versions of JavaScript, as shown in this table.

Event Handler for Submit Object	JavaScript Version	Bugs
onclick	JavaScript 1.0 and higher	Must return a value to work in Netscape 4 for Macintosh
onblur	JavaScript 1.0 and higher	Doesn't work with buttons in Netscape 3 and lower for Unix
onfocus	JavaScript 1.0 and higher	Doesn't work with buttons in Netscape 3 and lower for Unix

Event Handler for Submit Object	JavaScript Version	Bugs
onmousedown	JavaScript 1.2 and higher	
onmouseup	JavaScript 1.2 and higher	

Submit.value   The value property of a Submit object is initially set to the same value as the value attribute of the <INPUT> tag that defines the submit button in your HTML. This is the text that appears on the submit button.

Submit.value can be accessed in your JavaScript like this:

```
alert(document.myForm.mySubmit.value);
  // Alerts the value of the Submit
```

You can also change the value of a Submit object to any string in your JavaScript code. This changes the appearance of the button on the page.

```
document.myForm.mySubmit.value = "Don't Click Me!";
```

Submit.value is available in JavaScript 1.0 and higher.

Text

A text field is a single-line area where a user can type text into your form. Don't confuse this with a text area, which is discussed later in the chapter. The Text object provides access to the text field objects in your HTML page.

A Text object is defined on your page by inserting an <INPUT> tag with its type set to text in your HTML form. Although it's not required, it's a good idea to set a maxlength attribute in the <INPUT> tag to prevent people from using your form to overload your server. This is the maximum number or characters allowed in the field.

```
<form name="myForm">
  <input type="text" name="myText" value=
  "Type Here" maxlength="12"
    onClick="clicked()">
</form>
```

Text objects are available in JavaScript 1.0 and later.

Text.event   An event property of a Text object is initially set to the same value as an event handler property attribute of the <INPUT> tag that defines the text field in your HTML, such as onchange. The event handlers that can be defined for a text field are onblur, onchange, onfocus, and onselect.

An event property of a Text object should be equal to a function or equal to null, or you can simply not set one. If an event property is set to a function, that function will be executed when the event is performed. If an event property is set to null or not set, the text field will behave normally and no special code will be executed when an event is performed.

An event property of a Text object can be accessed in your JavaScript like this:

```
alert(document.myForm.myText.onchange);
    // Access onchange event property
    // Alerts function definition code
    // for user determined onchange function
    // This differs between IE and Netscape
```

You can change an event property with JavaScript in two ways. You can either assign a function literal to the event property, as here,

```
document.myForm.myText.onchange = function() { alert("New Function!"); };
    // Assigns a function literal
    // to the onchange property
```

or you can define a function and then assign it to an event property:

```
function functionChange()
{ alert("New Function!"); } // define new function
document.myForm.myText.onchange = functionChange;
    // Assigns a function to the onchange property
    // Note that no parentheses ()
are used when referencing the function
```

Different event properties are available to the Text object in different versions of JavaScript, as shown in the following table.

Event Handler for Text Object	JavaScript Version	Bugs
onblur	JavaScript 1.0 and higher	
onchange	JavaScript 1.0 and higher	

Event Handler for Text Object	JavaScript Version	Bugs
onfocus	JavaScript 1.0 and higher	
onselect	JavaScript 1.2 and higher	

Text.value   The `value` property of a Text object is initially set to the same value as the `value` attribute of the `<INPUT>` tag that defines the text field in your HTML. This is the text that appears in the text field.

`Text.value` can be accessed in your JavaScript like this:

```
alert(document.myForm.myText.value);
   // Alerts the value of the Text object
```

You can also change the value of a Text object to any string in your JavaScript code. This changes the appearance of the text field on the page.

```
document.myForm.myText.value = "Type your text here.";
```

`Text.value` is available in JavaScript 1.0 and higher.

Textarea

A text area is an area that is one or more lines long where a user can type text into your form. The Textarea object provides access to the text area objects in your HTML page.

A Textarea object is defined on your page by inserting a `<TEXTAREA>` tag into your HTML form. You should always close this tag.

```
<form name="myForm">
  <textarea name="myTextarea" onchange="changed()">
    The value of the textarea goes here.
  </textarea>
</form>
```

Textarea objects are available in JavaScript 1.0 and later.

Textarea.event   An event property of a Textarea object is initially set to the same value as an event handler property attribute of the `<TEXTAREA>` tag in your HTML, such as `onchange`. The event handlers that can be defined for a text area are `onblur`, `onchange`, `onfocus`, `onkeydown`, `onkeypress`, `onkeyup`, and `onselect`.

An event property of a Textarea object should be equal to a function or equal to `null`, or you can simply not set one. If an event property is set to a function, that function will be executed when the event is performed. If an event property is set to `null` or not set, the text area will behave normally and no special code will be executed when an event is performed.

An event property of a Textarea object can be accessed in your JavaScript like this:

```
alert(document.myForm.myTextarea.onchange);
   // Access onchange event property
   // Alerts function definition code
   // for user determined onchange function
   // This differs between IE and Netscape
```

You can change an event property with JavaScript in two ways. You can either assign a function literal to the event property, as here,

```
document.myForm.myTextarea.onchange = function() { alert("New Function!"); };
   // Assigns a function literal to the onchange property
```

or you can define a function and then assign it to an event property:

```
function functionChange() { alert("New Function!");
  } // define new function
       document.myForm.myTextarea.onchange=functionChange;
   // Assigns a function to the onchange property
   // Note that no parentheses () are used
   // when referencing the function
```

Different event properties are available to the Textarea object in different versions of JavaScript, as shown in the following table.

Event Handler for Textarea Object	JavaScript Version	Bugs
onblur	JavaScript 1.0 and higher	
onchange	JavaScript 1.0 and higher	
onfocus	JavaScript 1.0 and higher	
onkeydown	JavaScript 1.2 and higher	
onkeypress	JavaScript 1.2 and higher	

Event Handler for Textarea Object	JavaScript Version	Bugs
onkeyup	JavaScript 1.2 and higher	
onselect	JavaScript 1.2 and higher	

Textarea.value   The `value` property of a Textarea object is initially set to the value of the text between the `<TEXTAREA>` tags that define the text area in your HTML. This is the text that appears in the text area.

`Textarea.value` can be accessed in your JavaScript like this:

```
alert(document.myForm.myTextarea.value);
  // Alerts the value of the Textarea object
```

You can also change the `value` of a Textarea object to any string in your JavaScript code. This changes the appearance of the text area on the page.

```
document.myForm.myTextarea.value = "Type your text here.";
```

`Textarea.value` is available in JavaScript 1.0 and higher.

HTMLElement

HTMLElement refers to any HTML element be it `<A>`, `<BODY>`, or `<FORM>`, or others. The features such as `id` and `name` may be displayed by using some of the properties in this section.

HTMLElement.all[]   The `all[]` array of an HTMLElement object contains references to all the objects within an element in the order they appear in the HTML code.

The `all[]` array is commonly accessed in JavaScript code like this:

```
if (document.all)
    alert "Can use
    IE DHTML");
else alert("Can't use IE DHTML.");
  // testing for document.all can tell
    you whether you can use IE DHTML
```

You can use `all.length` to see how many objects are contained in an object.

```
alert("My document contains " + document.all.length + " objects");
  // alerts the number of objects
    contained in a document
```

HTMLElement.all[] is available in Internet Explorer 4 and higher.

HTMLElement.children[]   The children[] array contains references to all the objects that are contained directly in another element. For example, a form might contain a select menu that contains options; but the form doesn't directly contain the Option objects, only the actual Select object, so form.children[] contains only the Select object.

The children[] array can be accessed in your JavaScript code like this:

```
if (document.children) alert("The page
                              is not blank");
else alert("The page is blank");
  // testing whether a document is blank
```

You can use children.length to see how many objects are directly contained in an object.

```
alert("This document has " + document.children.length + " children");
// alerts the number of child objects in a document
```

HTMLElement.children[] is available in Internet Explorer 4 and higher.

HTMLElement.className   The className property is equal to the value of the class attribute of an HTML element. You can access class in your JavaScript code like this:

```
var bodyClass = document.body.className;
  // body class equals the value
  // of the class that the <body> is set to
```

You can also set the class to the name of any class you defined or imported with a style sheet, like this:

```
document.body.className = "redAndWhite";
  // change the <body> class to
  // the user-defined "redAndWhite" class
```

`HTMLElement.class` is available in Internet Explorer 4 and higher and Netscape 6.

HTMLElement.contains()   The `contains()` method returns a boolean value whether one object is contained within another. `HTMLElement.contains()` is available in Internet Explorer 4 and higher. For example,

```
<html>
<body>
<form name="login">
<input name="username" type="text">
<input name="password" type="password">
<input type="submit" value="submit">
</form>
<script type="text/javascript">
var formcheck =
document.body.contains(document.login);
var formelementcheck =
document.login.contains(document.login.username);
document.write(formcheck);
document.write(formelementcheck);
</script>
</body>
</html>
```

This returns `true` both times, because the `<BODY>` contains a `<FORM>` named `login` and the `<FORM>` named `login` contains an element called `username`.

HTMLElement.document   The `document` property contains a list of elements in the document. `HTMLElement.document` is available in Internet Explorer 4 and higher. For example,

```
<html>
<body>
<form name="login">
<input name="username" type="text">
<input name="password" type="password">
<input type="submit" value="submit">
</form>
<script type="text/javascript">
var formcheck = document.login;
if (formcheck) {
  document.write("form exists");
}
```

```
// This returns: form exists
</script>
</body>
</html>
```

HTMLElement.getAttribute()   The getAttribute() method returns an attribute for the requested element. It is available in IE 4+ and Netscape 6+.

```
<html>
<body>
<form name="login" type="text">
<input name="username" type="text">
<input name="password" type="password">
<input type="submit" value="submit">
</form>
<script type="text/javascript">
var attribute =
    document.login.password.getAttribute("type");
document.write(attribute);
</script>
</body>
</html>
```

This returns password, which is the type attribute from the password input element.

HTMLElement.id   The id property returns the id attribute, if it is set. It is available in IE 4+ and Netscape 6+.

```
<html>
<body>
<form name="login" type="text" id="form1">
<input name="username" type="text">
<input name="password" type="password">
<input type="submit" value="submit">
</form>
<script type="text/javascript">
var idname = document.login.id;
document.write(idname);
</script>
</body>
</html>
```

As you can see, this will return `form1`, which is the `id` of the `login` form.

HTMLElement.innerHTML   The `innerHTML` is quite handy, it returns the HTML that exists in the selected element. It is available in IE 4+ and Netscape 6+.

```
<html>
<body>
<form name="login" type="text">
<input name="username" type="text">
<input name="password" type="password">
<input type="submit" value="submit">
</form>
<script type="text/javascript">
var htmltest = document.login.innerHTML;
document.write(htmltest);
</script>
</body>
</html>
```

This returns the form above printed twice.

HTMLElement.innerText   The `innerText` property returns a string that appears within the requested element. It is available in IE 4+.

```
<html>
<body>
<p id="text">here is some text</p>
<script type="text/javascript">
var htmltest = window.text.innerText;
document.write(htmltest);
</script>
</body>
</html>
```

This returns the string `here is some text` two times.

HTMLElement.insertAdjacentHTML()   The `insertAdjacentHTML()` method inserts HTML adjacent to the requested element. It is available in IE 4+ only. The syntax is as follows:

```
HTMLElement.insertAdjacentHTML("location", "html");
```

The argument `html` refers to the HTML, that you would like to enter. The argument `location` refers to the location of the `html` argument. The possible locations are as follows:

Location	Description
BeforeBegin	Inserts the HTML before the beginning of the element
AfterBegin	Inserts the HTML after the beginning of the element
BeforeEnd	Inserts the HTML before the end of the element
AfterEnd	Inserts the HTML after the end of the element

HTMLElement.insertAdjacentText()   The `insertAdjacentText()` method inserts text adjacent to the requested element. It is available in IE 4+ only. The syntax is as follows:

```
HTMLElement.insertAdjacentHTML("location", "html");
```

The argument `html` refers to the HTML, that you would like to enter. The argument `location` refers to the location of the `html` argument. The possible locations are as follows:

Location	Description
BeforeBegin	Inserts the text before the beginning of the element
AfterBegin	Inserts the text after the beginning of the element
BeforeEnd	Inserts the text before the end of the element
AfterEnd	Inserts the text after the end of the element

HTMLElement.lang   The `lang` property specifies the `lang` attribute of the requested element. It is available in IE 4+.

```
<html>
<body>
<p id="text" lang="English">here is some text</p>
<script type="text/javascript">
var language = window.text.lang;
document.write(language);
</script>
</body>
</html>
```

This returns `English`, as you can see the `lang` attribute of the text paragraph is `English`.

HTMLElement.offsetHeight and HTMLElement.offsetWidth

The `offsetHeight` and `offsetWidth` properties return the height and width of the specified element and all of its content, in pixels. It is available in IE 4+.

```
<html>
<body>
<p id="text" lang="english">here is some text</p>
<script type="text/javascript">
var height = window.text.offsetHeight;
var width = window.text.offsetWidth;
document.write("Height: "+height+"<BR>Width: "+width);
</script>
</body>
</html>
```

This returns a line containing `Height: 19` followed by another line containing `Width: 331`.

HTMLElement.offsetLeft and HTMLElement.offsetTop

The `offsetLeft` and `offsetTop` properties return the x- and y-coordinates of the requested element. It is available in IE 4+.

```
<html>
<body>
<p id="text" lang="english">here is some text</p>
<script type="text/javascript">
var Left = window.text.offsetLeft;
var Top = window.text.offsetTop;
document.write("Left: " +Left+"<BR>Top: " +Top);
</script>
</body>
</html>
```

This returns a line containing `Left: 10` followed by another line containing `Top: 15`.

HTMLElement.offsetParent   The `offsetParent` property controls the parent class of the requested element. It is available in IE 4+.

```
<html>
<script LANGUAGE="Jscript">
function displayparent() {
  var tabled = document.all.thistd;
  alert("offsetParent: " + tabled.offsetParent.tagName);
}
```

```
</script>
<body onload="javascript:displayparent();">
<table border=1 >
<tr><td id="thistd">This is a small table</td></tr>
</table>
</body>
</html>
```

This displays an alert that reports offsetParent: TABLE, which is the parent of the thistd cell.

HTMLElement.outerHTML   The outerHTML property is used to replace the HTML within the requested element. It is available in IE 4+.

HTMLElement.outerText   The outerText property is used to replace the text within the requested element. It is available in IE 4+.

HTMLElement.parentElement   The parentElement property specifies the parent, which contains the requested element. It is available in IE 4+.

HTMLElement.removeAttribute()   The removeAttribute() method is used to remove a particular attribute from the specified element. It is available in Netscape 6+ and IE 4+. The syntax for this method is as follows:

```
HTMLElement.removeAttribute(attribute);
```

The attribute listed is the attribute that you wish to remove. This method will return true if the removal is successful, or false if not.

HTMLElement.scrollIntoView()   The scrollIntoView() method is used to scroll the browser to a particular element on the page. It is available in IE 4+. The syntax for this method is as follows:

```
HTMLElement.scrollIntoView(location);
```

The location argument is optional. You may specify top or bottom, to scroll the browser to the top or bottom of the page.

HTMLElement.setAttribute()   The setAttribute() method is used to set new attributes for the requested element. This method is available for IE 4+ and Netscape 6+. The syntax for this method is as follows:

```
HTMLElement.setAttribute(name, value);
```

The *name* argument refers to the name of the new attribute you are setting. The *value* argument refers to the value of the new attribute. Here's an example using a fictional <P> tag with the id of doctitle:

```
document.doctitle.setAttribute("align", "center");
```

This aligns the doctitle paragraph to the center.

HTMLElement.sourceIndex   The sourceIndex property determines the index of the specified element in the all[] array. It is available in IE 4+.

HTMLElement.style   The style property allows you to add or change the style sheet of the specified element. It is available in IE 4+ and Netscape 6+.

HTMLElement.tagName   The tagName property determines the name of the HTML tag for the specified element. It is available in IE 4+ and Netscape 6+.

HTMLElement.title   The title property allows you to add a *tool tip* for the specified element. This is similar to the *tool tips* in MS Windows, when you move your mouse over an icon on the desktop. It is available in IE 4+ and Netscape 6+.

document.forms[]

The forms[] array contains the Form objects, one for each form in the document. You may also use the length property as document.forms.length.

document.frames[]

The frames[] array contains an index of each <IFRAME>, floating frames contained in a document. You may call the IFRAME by name or element number. This property may also be used with the length property as document.frames.length.

document.getSelection

The getSelection method returns the text that is currently selected in the document. The text is removed from its HTML tags.

document.height

The height property contains the height, in pixels, of the current document.

document.images[]

The images[] array contains each Image object in the document. You may call an image by name or number in the array. You may also use the length property as document.images.length.

document.lastModified

The lastModified property contains the date and time of the last modification of the document.

document.links[]

The links[] property contains an array of each of the links contained in the document. You may call a link by name or element number. You may also use the length property as document.links.length.

document.mimeType

The mimeType property contains the MIME type of the current document.

document.open()

The open() method opens a stream to a document, so subsequent document.write() calls can append data to the document. You may also specify mimetype, so the browser knows how to handle the data. After using the open() and write() methods, you should use the close() method.

document.parentWindow

The parentWindow property returns a reference to the referenced document's parent window. For example, if documents are loaded into new windows, the `parentWindow` property could be interrogated to obtain a reference to the document's window, to then be able to manipulate that window.

document.queryCommandEnabled()

The `queryCommandEnabled` method allows you to determine whether a specific command (as defined by its command identifier) is available for the referenced object.

document.queryCommandIndeterm()

The `queryCommandIndeterm()` method can be used to determine whether a specific command is in the indeterminate state or not. It accepts one argument: a string value containing the command identifier in question.

document.queryCommandState()

The `queryCommandState()` method is used to determine the state of any command issued with the `execCommand` method (see above). It returns `true` if the command was successfully carried out on the referenced object, `false` if the command failed.

document.queryCommandSupported()

The `queryCommandSupported()` method can be used to determine whether the command is currently on or off. It accepts a single argument of a string value defining the command identifier to be queried and returns a boolean value of `true` if the command is on for the referenced object, or `false` if it isn't.

document.queryCommandText()

The `queryCommandText()` method can be used to determine the string associated with a command. It accepts the standard string argument of the command identifier together with a string value that can be either `Name` or `StatusText`. These, respectively, specify whether to return the short name of the command in question, or the status bar text that may appear with the specific command.

document.queryCommandValue()

The queryCommandValue() method can be used to determine the value argument used in the execCommand method. See the command identifiers for details of the values used with certain commands.

document.readyState

The readyState property contains the loading state of the document. It returns one of four values:

readyState Value	Description
uninitialized	The document has not started loading.
loading	The document is loading.
interactive	The document has loaded sufficiently for the user to interact with it.
complete	The document has completely loaded.

document.referrer

The referrer property contains the last URL the user clicked, if any.

document.scripts[]

The scripts[] property contains an array of each of the scripts contained in the document, where the [n] refers to the number of the requested script. You may also use the length property as document.scripts.length.

document.selection

The selection property contains a reference to any current document content that the user may have selected.

document.styleSheets[]

The styleSheets[] property contains a reference to any style sheets attached to the current document. You may call the style sheet by name or element number. You may also use the length property as document.styleSheets.length.

document.title

The title property contains the title of the current document.

document.URL

The URL property contains the URL of the current document.

document.width

The width property contains the width, in pixels, of the current document.

document.write()

The write() method can be used to write data (text, or any standard HTML) to a document.

document.writeln()

The writeln() method is essentially identical to the write method, except that it implies a line break after the string to write to the document. As line breaks are ignored by browsers though, the two methods tend to act identically.

Appendix

JavaScript Versions Chart

As we've discussed, JavaScript is not 100 percent compatible between versions of browsers. The following table lists compatibility information for common browsers as of the time of writing.

Browser	Platform	Browser Version	JavaScript Version	ECMA Support	Notes
Microsoft Internet Explorer	Windows	2.0	None	No	
		3.0	1.0	No	
		4.0	1.2	ECMA-262-	
		5.0	1.3	compliant	
		5.5	1.5	Full ECMAScript -262 Full ECMAScript-262	Uses JScript 5.5, which is compatible with ECMA-262 and supports most JavaScript 1.5 features
	Macintosh	5.0	1.3	Full	IE 4.x JavaScript
		4.0	1.2	ECMAScript-262	support on a Mac
		3.0	1.0	ECMA-262-	is poor at best.
		2.0	None	compliant No No	
	Unix	4.01	1.2	ECMA-262- compliant	HP-UX and Solaris only

Browser	Platform	Browser Version	JavaScript Version	ECMA Support	Notes
Netscape	Windows	2.0	1.0	None	Loss of support for
Navigator		3.0	1.1	None	some of NN 4.x
		4	1.2	None	JavaScript Gains
		4.7/4.5	1.3	Full	some of IE 5.x's
		6	1.5	ECMAScript-262 Full ECMAScript-262	proprietary features
	Macintosh	2.0	1.0	None	
		3.0	1.1	None	
		4.06	1.2	None	
		4.7/4.5	1.3	Full ECMAScript-262	
	Unix &	2.0	1.0	None	
	Linux	3.0	1.1	None	
		4.06	1.1	None	
	OS/2	2.02	None	None	
Opera	Windows	4.02	1.3	Full ECMAScript-262	
Mosaic	Windows	3.0	None	None	
	Macintosh	3.07	None	None	
America	Windows	3.0	1.0	None	Early versions of 3.x
Online					did not support
Browser		4.0	1.2	ECMA-262-	JavaScript.
		5.0	1.3	compliant Full ECMAScript-262	Pop-up windows disabled
	Macintosh	4.0	1.2	ECMA-262-	
		5.0	1.3	compliant Full ECMAScript-262	
MS	WebTV		1.1	None	
WebTV					

Character Charts

The three tables that follow describe the control, basic, and extended ASCII characters with their decimal, hexadecimal, octal, and HTML character representations. Most of the first 33 characters are not used very frequently; they are left over from teletype machines.

Aside from these characters, there are also Unicode characters, which include Greek, Hebrew, Arabic, Chinese, Braille, and other character sets. There are way too many for this book to cover; please refer to the official Unicode Character Charts, which are available in PDF format from http://www.unicode.org/charts/.

ASCII Control Character Chart

Decimal	Octal	Hex	Control Character	Character	Description
0	0	00	^@	NUL	Null
1	1	01	^A	SOH	Start of heading
2	2	02	^B	STX	Start of text
3	3	03	^C	ETX	End of text
4	4	04	^D	EOT	End of transmission
5	5	05	^E	ENQ	Enquiry
6	6	06	^F	ACK	Acknowledge
7	7	07	^G	BEL	Bell
8	10	08	^H	BS	Backspace
9	11	09	^I	HT	Horizontal tab
10	12	0A	^J	LF	Line feed - newline
11	13	0B	^K	VT	Vertical tab
12	14	0C	^L	FF	Form feed - new page
13	15	0D	^M	CR	Carriage return
14	16	0E	^N	SO	Shift out
15	17	0F	^O	SI	Shift in
16	20	10	^P	DLE	Data link escape
17	21	11	^Q	DC1	Device control 1
18	22	12	^R	DC2	Device control 2
19	23	13	^S	DC3	Device control 3
20	24	14	^T	DC4	Device control 4
21	25	15	^U	NAK	Negative acknowledge
22	26	16	^V	SYM	Synchronous idle
23	27	17	^W	ETB	End of transmission block
24	30	18	^X	CAN	Cancel
25	31	19	^Y	EM	End of medium
26	32	1A	^Z	SUB	Substitute
27	33	1B	^[	ESC	Escape
28	34	1C	^\	FS	File separator
29	35	1D	^]	GS	Group separator

A

Decimal	Octal	Hex	Control Character	Character	Description
30	36	1E	^^	RS	Record separator
31	37	1F	^_	US	Unit separator
32	40	20		SP	Space
127	177	7F	^?	DEL	Delete

Basic ASCII Character Chart

Decimal	Octal	Hex	HTML	Character
32	40	20		space
33	41	21		!
34	42	22	"	"
35	43	23		#
36	44	24		$
37	45	25		%
38	46	26	&	&
39	47	27		'
40	50	28		(
41	51	29		)
42	52	2A		*
43	53	2B		+
44	54	2C		,
45	55	2D		-
46	56	2E		.
47	57	2F		/
48	60	30		0
49	61	31		1
50	62	32		2
51	63	33		3
52	64	34		4
53	65	35		5
54	66	36		6
55	67	37		7
56	70	38		8
57	71	39		9
58	72	3A		:
59	73	3B		;
60	74	3C	<	<
61	75	3D		=
62	76	3E	>	>
63	77	3F		?
64	100	40		@

Decimal	Octal	Hex	HTML	Character
65	101	41		A
66	102	42		B
67	103	43		C
68	104	44		D
69	105	45		E
70	106	46		F
71	107	47		G
72	110	48		H
73	111	49		I
74	112	4A		J
75	113	4B		K
76	114	4C		L
77	115	4D		M
78	116	4E		N
79	117	4F		O
80	120	50		P
81	121	51		Q
82	122	52		R
83	123	53		S
84	124	54		T
85	125	55		U
86	126	56		V
87	127	57		W
88	130	58		X
89	131	59		Y
90	132	5A		Z
91	133	5B		[
92	134	5C		\
93	135	5D		]
94	136	5E	&circ;	^
95	137	5F		_
96	140	60		`
97	141	61		a
98	142	62		b
99	143	63		c
100	144	64		d
101	145	65		e
102	146	66		f
103	147	67		g
104	150	68		h
105	151	69		i

A

Decimal	Octal	Hex	HTML	Character
106	152	6A		j
107	153	6B		k
108	154	6C		l
109	155	6D		m
110	156	6E		n
111	157	6F		o
112	160	70		p
113	161	71		q
114	162	72		r
115	163	73		s
116	164	74		t
117	165	75		u
118	166	76		v
119	167	77		w
120	170	78		x
121	171	79		y
122	172	7A		z
123	173	7B		{
124	174	7C		|
125	175	7D		}
126	176	7E	˜	~
127	177	7F	&#127;	DEL

Extended ASCII Character Chart

Decimal	Octal	Hex	HTML	Character	Description
	200	80	€		Eurodollar (EUD)
129	201	81	[reserved]	[reserved]	[reserved]
130	202	82	‚	,	Low left rising single quote
131	203	83	ƒ	ƒ	Small italic f
132	204	84	„	„	Low left rising double quote
133	205	85	…	…	Low horizontal ellipsis
134	206	86	†	†	Dagger mark
135	207	87	‡	‡	Double dagger mark
136	210	88	ˆ	ˆ	Letter modifying circumflex
137	211	89	‰	‰	Per thousand (mille) sign

Decimal	Octal	Hex	HTML	Character	Description
138	212	8A	&Scaron;	Š	Capital S caron or hacek
139	213	8B	&lsaquo;	‹	Left single angle quote mark
140	214	8C	&OElig;	Œ	Capital OE ligature
141	215	8D	[reserved]	[reserved]	[reserved]
142	216	8E	[reserved]	[reserved]	[reserved]
143	217	8F	[reserved]	[reserved]	[reserved]
144	220	90	[reserved]	[reserved]	[reserved]
145	221	91	&lsquo;	'	Left single quotation mark
146	222	92	&#146;	'	Right single quote mark
147	223	93	&ldquo;	"	Left double quotation mark
148	224	94	&rdquo;	"	Right double quote mark
149	225	95	&bull;	Ã	Round filled bullet
150	226	96	&ndash;	–	En dash
151	227	97	&mdash;	—	Em dash
152	230	98	&#152;	˜	Small spacing tilde accent
153	231	99	&trade;	™	Trademark sign
154	232	9A	&scaron;	š	Small s caron or hacek
156	234	9C	&oelig;	œ	Small oe ligature
157	235	9D	[reserved]	[reserved]	[reserved]
158	236	9E	[reserved]	[reserved]	[reserved]
159	237	9F	&Yuml;	Ÿ	Capital Y dieresis or umlaut
160	240	A0			Non-breaking space
161	241	A1	&iexcl;	¡	Inverted exclamation mark
162	242	A2	&cent;	¢	Cent sign
163	243	A3	&pound;	£	Pound sterling sign
164	244	A4	&curren;	¤	General currency sign

A

Decimal	Octal	Hex	HTML	Character	Description
165	245	A5	¥	¥	Yen sign
166	246	A6	¦	¦	Broken vertical bar
167	247	A7	§	§	Section sign
168	250	A8	¨	¨	Spacing dieresis or umlaut
169	251	A9	©	©	Copyright sign
170	252	AA	ª	ª	Feminine ordinal indicator
171	253	AB	«		Left (double) angle quote
172	254	AC	¬	¬	Logical not sign
173	255	AD	­		Soft hyphen
174	256	AE	®	®	Registered trademark sign
175	257	AF	¯	¯	Spacing macron (long)
176	260	B0	°	°	Degree sign
177	261	B1	±	±	Plus-or-minus sign
178	262	B2	²	^{2}	Superscript 2
179	263	B3	³	^{3}	Superscript 3
180	264	B4	´	´	Spacing acute accent
181	265	B5	µ	µ	Micro sign
182	266	B6	¶	¶	Paragraph sign, pilcro
183	267	B7	·	·	Middle dot
184	270	B8	¸	¸	Spacing cedilla
185	271	B9	¹	^{1}	Superscript 1
186	272	BA	º	º	Masculine ordinal indicator
187	273	BB	»		Right (double) angle q
188	274	BC	¼	¼	Fraction 1/4
189	275	BD	½	½	Fraction 1/2
190	276	BE	¾	¾	Fraction 3/4
191	277	BF	¿	¿	Inverted question mark
192	300	C0	À	À	Capital A grave
193	301	C1	Á	Á	Capital A acute

Decimal	Octal	Hex	HTML	Character	Description
194	302	C2	Â	Â	Capital A circumflex
195	303	C3	Ã	Ã	Capital A tilde
196	304	C4	Ä	Ä	Capital A dieresis or umlaut
197	305	C5	Å	Å	Capital A ring
198	306	C6	Æ	Æ	Capital AE ligature
199	307	C7	Ç	Ç	Capital C cedilla
200	310	C8	È	È	Capital E grave
201	311	C9	É	É	Capital E acute
202	312	CA	Ê	Ê	Capital E circumflex
203	313	CB	Ë	Ë	Capital E dieresis or umlaut
204	314	CC	Ì	Ì	Capital I grave
205	315	CD	Í	Í	Capital I acute
206	316	CE	Î	Î	Capital I circumflex
207	317	CF	Ï	Ï	Capital I dieresis or umlaut
208	320	D0	Ð	Ð	Capital ETH
209	321	D1	Ñ	Ñ	Capital N tilde
210	322	D2	Ò	Ò	Capital O grave
211	323	D3	Ó	Ó	Capital O acute
212	324	D4	Ô	Ô	Capital O circumflex
213	325	D5	Õ	Õ	Capital O tilde
214	326	D6	Ö	Ö	Capital O dieresis or umlaut
215	327	D7	×	×	Multiplication sign
216	330	D8	Ø	Ø	Capital O slash
217	331	D9	Ù	Ù	Capital U grave
218	332	DA	Ú	Ú	Capital U acute
219	333	DB	Û	Û	Capital U circumflex
220	334	DC	Ü	Ü	Capital U dieresis or umlaut

A

Decimal	Octal	Hex	HTML	Character	Description
221	335	DD	&Yacute;	Ý	Capital Y acute
222	336	DE	&THORN;	Þ	Capital THORN
223	337	DF	&szlig;	ß	Small sharp s, sz ligature
224	340	E0	&agrave;	à	Small a grave
225	341	E1	&aacute;	á	Small a acute
226	342	E2	&acirc;	â	Small a circumflex
227	343	E3	&atilde;	ã	Small a tilde
228	344	E4	&auml;	ä	Small a dieresis or umlaut
229	345	E5	&aring;	å	Small a ring
230	346	E6	&aelig;	æ	Small ae ligature
231	347	E7	&ccedil;	ç	Small c cedilla
232	350	E8	&egrave;	è	Small e grave
233	351	E9	&eacute;	é	Small e acute
234	352	EA	&ecirc;	ê	Small e circumflex
235	353	EB	&euml;	ë	Small e dieresis or umlaut
236	354	EC	&igrave;	ì	Small i grave
237	355	ED	&iacute;	í	Small i acute
238	356	EE	&icirc;	î	Small i circumflex
239	357	EF	&iuml;	ï	Small i dieresis or umlaut
240	360	F0	&eth;	ð	Small eth
241	361	F1	&ntilde;	ñ	Small n tilde
242	362	F2	&ograve;	ò	Small o grave
243	363	F3	&oacute;	ó	Small o acute
244	364	F4	&ocirc;	ô	Small o circumflex
245	365	F5	&otilde;	õ	Small o tilde
246	366	F6	&ouml;	ö	Small o dieresis or umlaut
247	367	F7	&divide;	÷	Division sign
248	370	F8	&oslash;	ø	Small o slash
249	371	F9	&ugrave;	ù	Small u grave
250	372	FA	&uacute;	ú	Small u acute
251	373	FB	&ucirc;	û	Small u circumflex

Decimal	Octal	Hex	HTML	Character	Description
252	374	FC	ü	ü	Small u dieresis or umlaut
253	375	FD	ý	ý	Small y acute
254	376	FE	þ	þ	Small thorn
255	377	FF	ÿ	ÿ	Small y dieresis or umlaut

Event Handlers Chart

This table describes the JavaScript event handlers, the elements they are used with, their JavaScript compatibility, and common bugs. Each event handler is discussed in Chapter 5.

A

Event Handler	Elements	JavaScript Version	Bugs
onAbort	Image	JavaScript 1.1	None
onBlur	Window, all other elements	JavaScript 1.0	This handler's usage with the Window object is new in JavaScript 1.1.
onChange	Select menu, text input elements	JavaScript 1.0	None
onClick	Links, buttons	JavaScript 1.0	onClick must return true to work properly on Netscape for Macs.
onDblClick	Document, link, image, buttons	JavaScript 1.2	Doesn't work in Netscape 4 on Mac or Unix platforms
onDragDrop	Document	JavaScript 1.2	Netscape 4+ only
onError	Image	JavaScript 1.1	None
onFocus	Text elements, window, all other form elements	JavaScript 1.0	This handler's usage with the Window object and with form elements other than text input field is new in JavaScript 1.1.

Event Handler	Elements	JavaScript Version	Bugs
onKeyDown	Document, image, link, text elements	JavaScript 1.2	This handler's usage with anything but text input fields is not supported by Netscape 4 on Unix platforms.
onKeyPress	Document, image, link, text elements	JavaScript 1.2	This handler's usage with anything but text input fields is not supported by Netscape 4 on Unix platforms.
onKeyUp	Document, image, link, text elements	JavaScript 1.2	This handler's usage with anything but text input fields is not supported by Netscape 4 on Unix platforms.
onLoad	Window, image	JavaScript 1.0	This handler's usage with an image element is new in JavaScript 1.1.
onMouseDown	Document, link, image, buttons	JavaScript 1.2	This handler's usage with button elements is not supported in Netscape 4 on Unix platforms.
onMouseOut	Link, image, layer	JavaScript 1.1	This handler's usage with image elements is new in JavaScript 1.2 and is not supported by Netscape 4 on Unix platforms. Its compatibility with Layer objects is new in JavaScript 1.2.

Event Handler	Elements	JavaScript Version	Bugs
onMouseOver	Link, image, layer	JavaScript 1.0	This handler's usage with image elements is new in JavaScript 1.2 and is not supported by Netscape 4 on Unix platforms. Its compatibility with Layer objects is new in JavaScript 1.2.
onMouseUp	Document, link, image, button	JavaScript 1.2	This handler's compatibility with button elements is not compatible with Netscape 4 on Unix platforms.
onReset	Form	JavaScript 1.1	None
onResize	Window	JavaScript 1.2	None
onSubmit	Form	JavaScript 1.1	None
onUnload	Window	JavaScript 1.0	None

A

The Authors' Bookmarks

Here are a few of our favored web sites for JavaScript and web development information:

- **Whatis.com** (http://www.whatis.com)   This site is probably best described as an encyclopedia of practically everything that has to do with information technology. It currently contains around 3,000 entries and many valuable "Fast Reference Pages."

- **CNET's Regular Expression Builder** (http://builder.cnet.com/ webbuilding/pages/Programming/Kahn/050698/toolrei.html) This invaluable tool will help you create, check, and simplify your regular expressions.

- **The JavaScript Source** (http://www.javascriptsource.com) This is a repository of JavaScript, with scripts that range from games, to calendars, to navigation, to forms.

- **The World Wide Web Consortium** (http://www.w3c.org) This excellent reference site controls the standards of HTML, XML, CSS, and over 25 other web mark-up languages.

- **Glassdog's Web Design** (http://www.glassdog.com/ design-o-rama/ index.shtml) Lance Arthur has several nice tutorials on HTML, JavaScript, style sheets, and design. This site is definitely worth a look!

- **Netscape DevEdge** (http://developer.netscape.com/) This is Netscape's repository of tools for web developers, which includes the white papers for JavaScript and ECMAScript.

- **MSDN Library** (http://msdn.microsoft.com/) Microsoft's library of their programming languages also includes the white papers for Internet Explorer and its features.

- **Internet Explorer Web Accessories** (http:// www.microsoft .com/Windows/IE/WebAccess/default.asp) Microsoft's web accessory page has one extremely useful tool, the *Microsoft Web Developer Accessories*. It includes two tools the first is a DOM viewer, which allows you to step through the entire DOM of any page. The other tool is a partial source viewer, which allows you to highlight a section of HTML and view the source. The *Microsoft Web Developer Accessories* package is currently the last item on that page.

- **CAST: Bobby** (http://www.cast.org/bobby) Use this site to determine whether your pages are accessible for the handicapped. It generates a very detailed site report. You can also get a downloadable version, to test intranet sites.

- **SourceForge** (http://www.sourceforge.org) This service for Open Source developers is a community of developers and users, where you can develop Open Source software on a platform for free.

- **Perl Monks** (http://www.perlmonks.com) This isn't a JavaScript site, but if you are using the Perl programming language, this site has a great community, where you can go to gather information and ask questions. It has good information on regular expressions too.

Web Browsers

Here are the URLs for several web browsers, which you may be interested in trying out.

- Netscape Navigator at http://home.netscape.com/ download/ index.html; current platforms: Windows, Macintosh, and Linux.
- Internet Explorer at http://www.microsoft.com/ie; current platform: Windows
- Internet Explorer at http://www.microsoft.com/ unix/ie/ default.asp; current platform: Unix (Solaris and HP-UX)
- Mozilla at http://www.mozilla.org; current platforms: Windows, Macintosh, and Linux
- Opera at http://www.opera.com; current platform: Windows only
- Lynx Text-Only Browser at http://lynx.browser.org/; current platforms: Unix, Linux, Windows, VMS, DOS, and OS/2
- iCab at http://www.icab.de/; current platform: Macintosh only
- Konqueror at http://www.konqueror.org/; current platform: Linux only
- NCSA Mosaic at http://archive.ncsa.uiuc.edu/ SDG/Software/ XMosaic/; current platform: Linux and various flavors of Unix
- NCSA Mosaic at http://archive.ncsa.uiuc.edu/ SDG/ Software/ mosaic-w/releaseinfo/; current platform: Windows

A

Country Codes

Mentioned in several of the chapters are country codes, which may be used to determine the language of the client's browser or operating system. This table includes all the current country codes.

Country Code	Country	Country Code	Country
af	Afrikaans	ar	Arabic
ar-ae	Arabic (U.A.E.)	ar-bh	Arabic (Bahrain)
ar-dz	Arabic (Algeria)	ar-eg	Arabic (Egypt)
ar-iq	Arabic (Iraq)	ar-jo	Arabic (Jordan)
ar-kw	Arabic (Kuwait)	ar-lb	Arabic (Lebanon)

Country Code	Country	Country Code	Country
ar-ly	SArabic (Libya)	ar-ma	Arabic (Morocco)
ar-om	Arabic (Oman)	ar-qa	Arabic (Qatar)
ar-sa	Arabic (Saudi Arabia)	ar-sy	Arabic (Syria)
ar-tn	Arabic (Tunisia)	ar-ye	Arabic (Yemen)
be	Belarusian	bg	Bulgarian
ca	Catalan	cs	Czech
da	Danish	de	German (Germany)
de-at	German (Austria)	de-ch	German (Switzerland)
de-li	German (Liechtenstein)	de-lu	German (Luxembourg)
el	Greek	en	English
en-au	English (Australia)	en-bz	English (Belize)
en-ca	English (Canada)	en-gb	English (United Kingdom)
en-ie	English (Ireland)	en-jm	English (Jamaica)
en-nz	English (New Zealand)	en-tt	English (Trinidad)
en-us	English (United States)	en-za	English (South Africa)
es	Spanish (Traditional Sort)	es	Spanish (International Sort)
es-ar	Spanish (Argentina)	es-bo	Spanish (Bolivia)
es-cl	Spanish (Chile)	es-co	Spanish (Colombia)
es-cr	Spanish (Costa Rica)	es-do	Spanish (Dominican Republic)
es-ec	Spanish (Ecuador)	es-gt	Spanish (Guatemala)
es-hn	Spanish (Honduras)	es-mx	Spanish (Mexico)
es-ni	Spanish (Nicaragua)	es-pa	Spanish (Panama)
es-pe	Spanish (Peru)	es-pr	Spanish (Puerto Rico)
es-py	Spanish (Paraguay)	es-sv	Spanish (El Salvador)
es-uy	Spanish (Uruguay)	es-ve	Spanish (Venezuela)

Country Code	Country	Country Code	Country
et	Estonian	eu	Basque
fa	Farsi	fi	Finnish
fo	Faeroese	fr	French (France)
fr-be	French (Belgium)	fr-ca	French (Canada)
fr-ch	French (Switzerland)	fr-lu	French (Luxembourg)
gd	Gaelic	he	Hebrew
hi	Hindi	hr	Croatian
hu	Hungarian	in	Indonesian
is	Icelandic	it	Italian (Italy)
it-ch	Italian (Switzerland)	ja	Japanese
ji	Yiddish	ko	Korean
lt	Lithuanian	lv	Latvian
mk	Macedonian (FYROM)	ms	Malay (Malaysia)
mt	Maltese	nl	Dutch (Netherlands)
nl-be	Dutch (Belgium)	no	Norwegian (Bokmal)
no	Norwegian (Nynorsk)	pl	Polish
pt	Portuguese (Portugal)	pt-br	Portuguese (Brazil)
rm	Rhaeto-Romanic	ro	Romanian
ro-mo	Romanian (Moldova)	ru	Russian
ru-mo	Russian (Moldova)	sb	Sorbian
sk	Slovak	sl	Slovenian
sq	Albanian	sr	Serbian (Latin)
sr	Serbian (Cyrillic)	sv	Swedish
sv-fi	Swedish (Finland)	sx	Sutu
th	Thai	tn	Tswana
tr	Turkish	ts	Tsonga
uk	Ukrainian	ur	Urdu
vi	Vietnamese	xh	Xhosa
zh	Chinese	zh-cn	Chinese (PRC)
zh-hk	Chinese (Hong Kong)	zh-sg	Chinese (Singapore)
zh-tw	Chinese (Taiwan)	zu	Zulu

A

JavaScript Security

Because JavaScript is most commonly used with web pages, security is an important consideration for JavaScript coders. There are many general security pitfalls that are inherent in every kind of web application regardless of which programming language is used when it comes to sensitive information. These pitfalls include storing sensitive information without encryption, using an inadequate encryption method, and storing sensitive information in a way that it is available to members of the "outside world."

JavaScript's Inherent Security

A long-running joke is that big software companies such as Microsoft and AOL like to pitch their product's *limitations* as *features*. In the case of JavaScript, however, its limitations are advantageous when it comes to security.

Client-side JavaScript can't read, write, modify, move, or delete files from the user's computer, with the exception of a page's own cookie files. (For more information about browser cookies, see the "Cookies" section in Chapter 5, "Client-side JavaScript.") And for good reason—these are things that every paranoid user fears the most.

The other thing that every paranoid user fears is a web page will send private information back to the Web. There are two reasons not to be as concerned about this in the case of JavaScript programs.

First, the only information that JavaScript can technically get from a user's computer is arbitrary information about which browser, operating system, and IP address the user is using, in addition to any information that the users provides intentionally. This information is accessible not only to JavaScript programs but to any web-based program.

Second, JavaScript isn't able to communicate directly with a web server all by itself. The only networking capability that JavaScript has at all is its ability to retrieve a web page or submit a form.

Security by Obscurity Doesn't Work

The most common security hole in JavaScript applications occurs when sensitive information is stored either in the source code of a web document or in a cookie on the user's computer. Either technique relies on "security by obscurity," which occurs most frequently when a coder assumes that no users on his or her web page are smart enough to view either the source code or the cookies on the their own computer. This assumption is increasingly false, and "security by obscurity" is totally inadequate and should be avoided in all but two scenarios.

The first scenario is when the information that you'd like to store is totally inconsequential or public, such the fact that the user's favorite color is blue or that Berlin is the capital of Germany. Neither of these tidbits of information is sensitive in the first place and needn't be guarded carefully. Note that a user's password that is needed to access even the most inconsequential information doesn't fall into this category, because users often have the same login name and password for many different things.

A

The second scenario is when the site you're working in is actually a secure intranet site. Unlike on an Internet site, on an intranet site both web pages and the computers that view them are actively guarded from the outside world.